Math
Volume 1

Grades K-2

Published by Ideal School Supply
an imprint of

Author: Jill Osofsky
Editor: Karen Thompson

Children's Publishing

Published by Ideal School Supply
An imprint of McGraw-Hill Children's Publishing
Copyright © 2004 McGraw-Hill Children's Publishing

Send all inquiries to:
McGraw-Hill Children's Publishing
3195 Wilson Drive NW
Grand Rapids, Michigan 49544

Funtastic Frogs™ Math Volume 1—grades K-2
ISBN: 0-7424-2770-6

1 2 3 4 5 6 7 8 9 MAL 09 08 07 06 05 04

Table of Contents

About This Book

This book is one in a series of books designed to develop children's mathematical thinking, scientific thought process skills, and problem solving abilities. Each book supports the use of *Funtastic Frogs™* Counters in activities that teach key concepts.

Funtastic Frogs™ Counters are available in six different colors: green, blue, yellow, green, red, and orange; and in three sizes; 3 grams, 6 grams, and 12 grams. A unique lacing feature allows children to use the frogs in a wide range of counting and patterning activities.

As children use and manipulate the fun-to-hold *Funtastic Frogs™* Counters along with the reproducible activities in this book, they will explore units in Matching and Sorting, Counting and Numbers, Balancing Numbers, Measuring, and Making Patterns. Each unit is numbered and labeled throughout and is ideal as a handy reference by busy teachers. Each separate unit focuses on a specific skill. There are Teacher's Notes for each unit that includes a list of materials, mathematical content, and a skills chart; as well as Sample Solutions, Activity Guides, and Reproducible Photocopy Master Pages.

Use this book and all the books in the series to extend and enrich your math and science programs. These excellent resources are perfect additions to your classroom to be used for learning centers, for large and small cooperative groups, or for individual and independent discovery. This book is excellent for home schooling, as well as anyone interested in helping young students get a head start in math. The books support the recommendations as stated in the *NCTM Standards*.

Funtastic Frogs™ activity books and *Funtastic Frogs™* Counters and *Logs™* are available from Ideal School Supply, any Ideal School Supply Dealer, or our website at www.MHteachers.com.

Funtastic FROGS™

Matching & Sorting

Unit 1

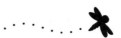

Teacher's Notes for This Unit

In Unit I, *Matching & Sorting*, children will use the frog counters in activities to:
- sort and match objects according to color and size
- sort objects into groups or sets that are alike
- find groups or sets that are the *same*
- compare groups or sets to find which has *more* or *fewer*
- find relationships between groups or sets
- sort objects using Venn diagrams
- observe relationships to make a sorting rule
- find objects that belong to more than one group or set

The activities in this unit are designed to develop children's matching, sorting, and classifying skills using the attributes of color and size. Learning to match, sort, and classify objects and organize data will help children develop their logical thinking and reasoning skills. The activities in this unit support current mathematics standards and lay the foundation for higher-level mathematics skills in later years.

Contents

This unit contains 20 activities divided into sections. Each section contains five similar activities, giving children the opportunity to practice and use each skill. The book also includes a game that allows children to apply what they have learned about matching and sorting.

Sample solutions are provided on pages 12 and 13. A photocopy master for the frog counters is also included on page 14.

Math Skills and Understandings	Related Activities
Match, sort, and classify objects	Activities 1–20
Sort and classify objects using different attributes	Activities 1–20
Use concrete and pictorial representations of numerical situations	Activities 1–20
Use one-to-one correspondence to develop number concepts	Activities 1–15
Describe how objects are alike and how they are different	Activities 6–20
Explore the concept of groups or sets	Activities 11–15
Sort and compare sets of concrete objects to find which has *more, fewer,* or the *same*	Activities 11–15
Sort objects to make generalizations about relationships	Activities 6–20
Sort objects in more than one way	Activities 1–20
Represent data using Venn diagrams	Activities 16–20

Suggestions for Classroom Use

The activities are sequenced by level of difficulty within each section and from section to section. Modify a section if you find it is too challenging for your children, or not challenging enough.

The activities can be introduced to the whole group using an overhead projector, the chalkboard, or sitting in a circle on the floor. Once children understand the directions for the activities, they can work in pairs, small groups, or individually at a learning center.

Encourage children to talk about their thinking and discoveries. Talking helps them clarify their thoughts and allows others to hear how they might solve the same problem a different way.

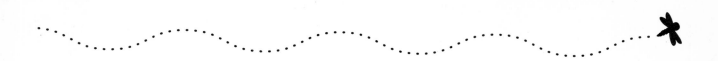

When you introduce a section of the unit, lead the children through the first activity in that section. Discuss the directions and how to record their work. You can use yarn for the sorting circles and Venn diagrams pictured on the activity pages, along with sentence strips for writing the sorting rules. When reviewing an activity with the group, encourage the children to talk about their discoveries.

Mathematical Content by Section

Activities 1–5: Matching by color and size. Children are introduced to the vocabulary associated with matching. First they match the colors, then the sizes of the frogs indicated on each picture and circle the frogs that are the same. They also match frogs in a scene. They match the frogs to complete patterns. *Make a Match* is a game for two players that reinforces the skills in the section.

Activities 6–10: Sort objects to find which are alike and which are different then observe relationships to make a sorting rule. Encourage the children to name and describe sets or groups of frogs. Demonstrate how they can sort frogs of mixed sizes and colors. Sort for the attribute *small*. Explain that you want to use the sorting rule *small frogs*. Point out that small frogs match the rule and belong in the circle, and all other frogs belong outside the circle. Ask questions such as: *Why does this frog belong in the circle? How are the frogs inside the circle alike? How can we label the circle? How are the frogs outside the circle different from the frogs inside?* Ask small groups to find a different way to sort the frogs, then record their rule, and show their results. Continue in the same way throughout the section. Demonstrate, then assign the activity pages. For Activities 8–10, remind children to start by matching the frogs on the sheet with their frog counters.

Activities 11–15: Comparing to find which groups of frogs have *more*, *fewer*, or the *same*. Place five red frogs in one circle. Then place five purple frogs in another circle. Ask: *Do you think there are as many red frogs as purple frogs? How can we find out?* Guide children to discover that frogs can be matched by arranging them in pairs, one to one, to compare the amounts. Children complete Activity 11 in pairs. Children use the same match-and-compare technique to find which group has *more* in Activity 12, *fewer* for Activity 13, and *more*, *fewer*, or the *same* for Activity 14.

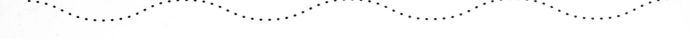

Materials

You may wish to make an overhead transparency of the first activity page in each section as an introduction to the activities that follow.

For each pupil, pair of children, or group, you will need:
- pencils
- crayons or colored markers to match the colors of the frogs
- a tub of frog counters in three sizes and six colors
- an activity page for each child or pair of children

Note that Activity 15 requires small resealable plastic bags that can hold 12 small frog counters.

If children are not able to record by writing numbers and coloring, make copies of page 14. The children can color and cut out the frogs, then paste or glue them in place to record.

Introducing the Activities

Encourage the children to compare the frogs and tell how they are alike and how they are different. Ask them to find different ways of sorting or grouping the frogs. Have them describe the different sizes and weights.

This exploration prior to beginning the activities provides an opportunity to introduce vocabulary used throughout the unit. Introduce terms such as *alike*, *different*, *more than*, *fewer than*, and *groups* or *sets* informally. Use the terms that are appropriate for your children. It is also a good time to introduce the symbols that will appear on some activity pages. The frogs' sizes are referred to as *small*, *medium*, and *large*. The color for each frog is represented by the lowercase first letter of each color word on the front of the frog. Be sure all children are familiar with these terms before you begin instruction.

For Activity 15, children use estimation to guess which set of frogs has *more* members. Put 12 small frogs—eight of one color and four of another—in a resealable plastic bag. Children estimate whether there are *more* or *fewer* frogs of one color than the other. They record their guesses, then open the bag, count, and compare the colors to find which has *more* and which has *fewer*. Demonstrate how to fill in the blanks on the activity page. Distribute bags of frogs to small groups. Have each group repeat the activity and record the results.

Activities 16–20: Sorting by size and color using a Venn Diagram; use logical reasoning to solve problems. Activity 16 introduces the Venn diagram. Make two circles and label them *large* and *red*. Model placing frogs where they match the rules. When you place frogs that match both rules, explain that they belong in the intersection of the two circles—the place where the circles overlap. Ask: *Where do the red frogs belong? Where do the large frogs belong? Where do the large red frogs belong?* Repeat the activity using different sorting rules.

Introduce the remaining activities in the same way. Children place the frogs where they belong according to the rules. In the final activity, children supply the rules.

The Match Game. This two player game is designed to give children additional practice in sorting and matching. Players take turns putting a frog on the game board. On each turn, the player must place a frog next to, above, or below a frog that matches it in color or size. The last player to correctly place a frog is the winner.

Sample Solutions for This Unit

These are sample solutions. Additional solutions are possible for some activities.

Activity

1A.   **1B.**   **1C.**

2A. small frogs **2B.** medium frogs **2C.** large frogs

3

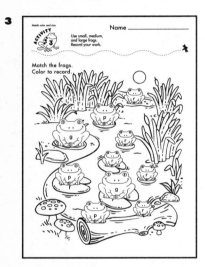

4B.   **4C.**   **4D.**

5 Answers will vary.

6

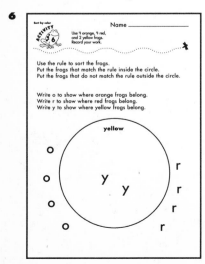

Activity

7

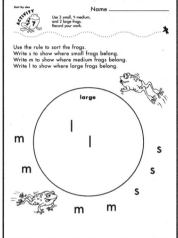

8

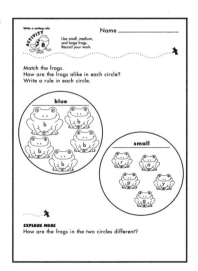

EXPLORE MORE The frogs differ in size and color.

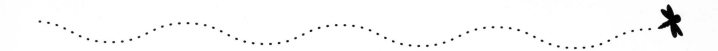

Sample Solutions

These are sample solutions. Additional solutions are possible for some activities.

Activity

9

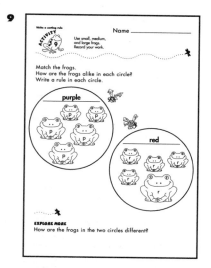

EXPLORE MORE The frogs are different colors.

10

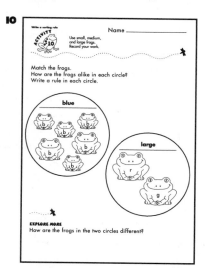

EXPLORE MORE The frogs differ in size and color.

Activity

11B. Each circle has medium frogs.

12B. There are more small frogs.

13B. There are fewer medium frogs.

14B. The number of frogs in each circle is the same.

15 Answers will vary based on the colors used and children's estimates. There will be 8 of 1 color and 4 of the other.

16 2 small yellow frogs

17 4 small blue frogs

18

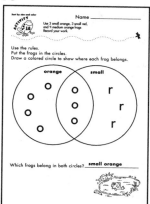

19

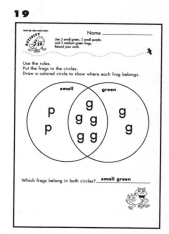

20

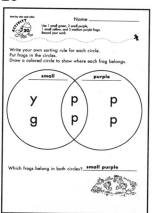

14

ACTIVITY 3

Use small, medium, and large frogs. Record your work.

Name _____

Match the frogs.
Color to record.

Use small frogs.
Record your work.

Name _____

Match the frogs to make each row the same.
Find the missing color for each row.
Color to record.

A. p   y   g   o

B. p   g   o

C.  p   y   o

D. p   

Use small, medium, and large frogs.

Name _____

Make a Match Game

READY Take 8 frogs of any color and size.
Decide who goes first.
The first player to reach the last square is the winner.

PLAY The first player puts any frog on START.
Take turns. On each turn put a frog in the next square that matches the color **or** size of the frog in the square before it. If you can't make a match, your turn is over.

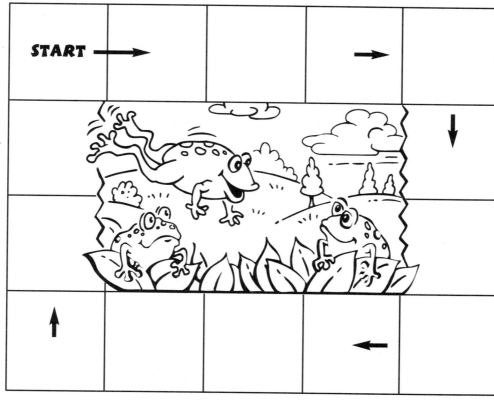

DO MORE
Sort the frogs into groups that are alike.

Use 4 orange, 4 red, and 2 yellow frogs. Record your work.

Name _____

Use the rule to sort the frogs.
Put the frogs that match the rule inside the circle.
Put the frogs that do not match the rule outside the circle.

Write o to show where orange frogs belong.
Write r to show where red frogs belong.
Write y to show where yellow frogs belong.

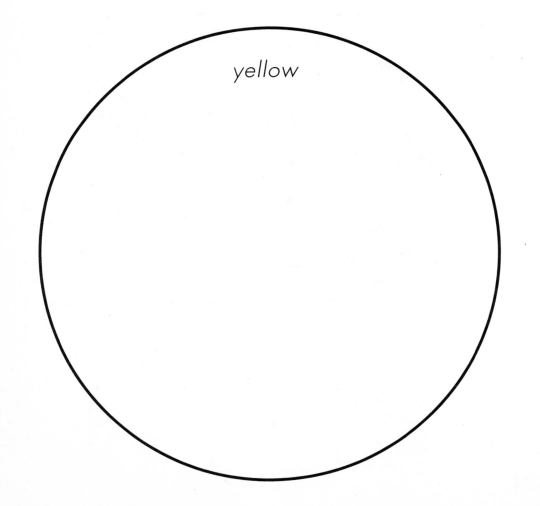

yellow

ACTIVITY 7

Name _____

Use 3 small, 4 medium,
and 2 large frogs.
Record your work.

Use the rule to sort the frogs.
Write s to show where small frogs belong.
Write m to show where medium frogs belong.
Write l to show where large frogs belong.

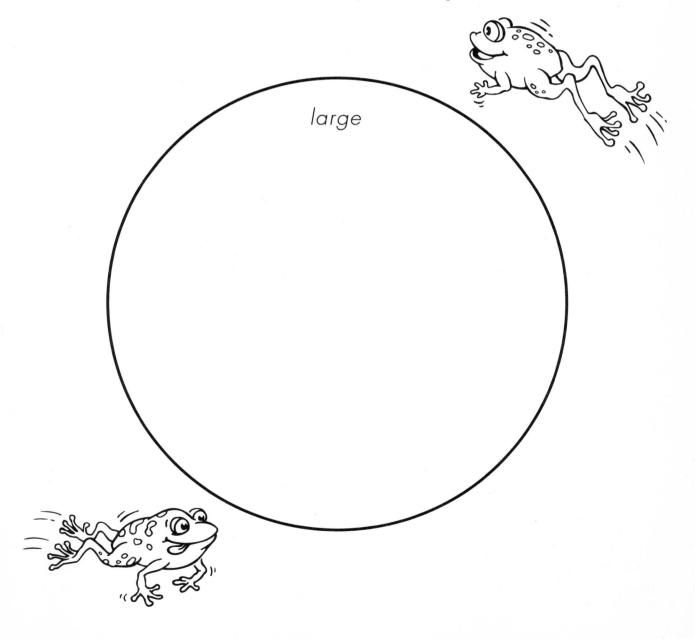

large

Use small, medium, and large frogs. Record your work.

Name _____

Match the frogs.
How are the frogs alike in each circle?
Write a rule in each circle.

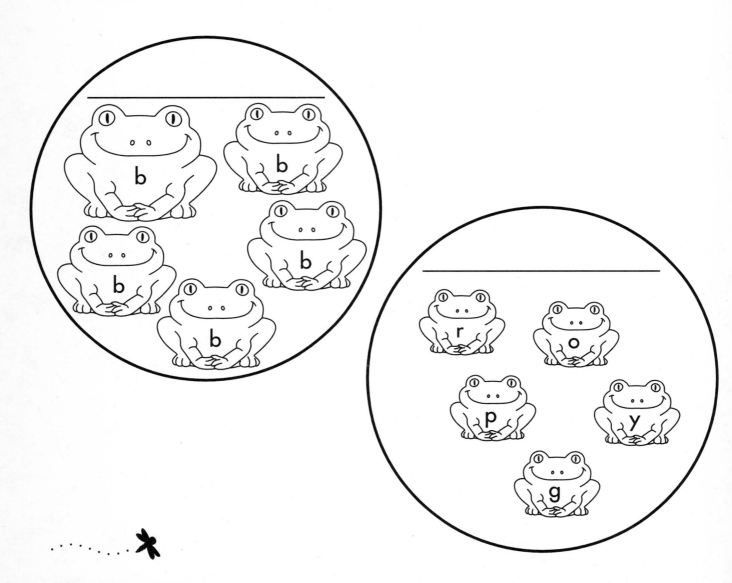

EXPLORE MORE

How are the frogs in the two circles different?

Use small, medium, and large frogs. Record your work.

Name _____

Match the frogs.
How are the frogs alike in each circle?
Write a rule in each circle.

EXPLORE MORE

How are the frogs in the two circles different?

Use small, medium,
and large frogs.
Record your work.

Name _____

Match the frogs.
How are the frogs alike in each circle?
Write a rule in each circle.

EXPLORE MORE

How are the frogs in the two circles different?

Use small and medium frogs. Record your work.

Name _____

A. Match the frogs.
How are the frogs in each circle the same?

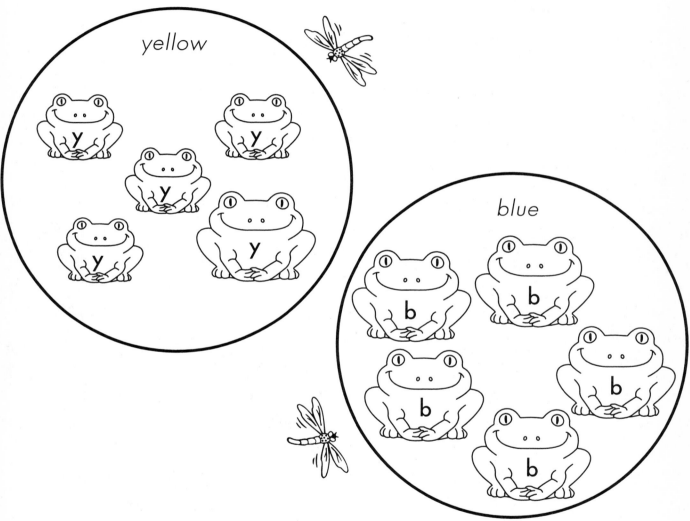

yellow

blue

B. Circle the correct sentence.

Each circle has small frogs.

Each circle has medium frogs.

Compare sets to find which has more

ACTIVITY 12

Use small and medium frogs.
Record your work.

Name _____

A. Match the frogs.
Which circle has more frogs?

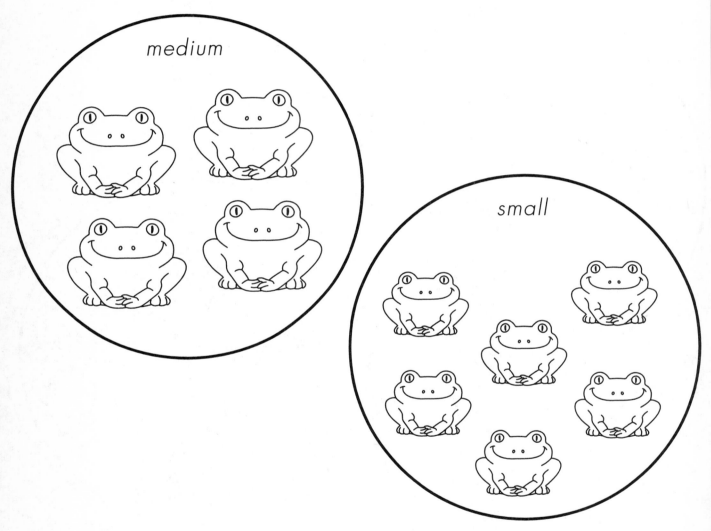

medium

small

B. Circle the correct sentence.

There are more small frogs.

There are more medium frogs.

© McGraw-Hill Children's Publishing   **26**   0-7424-2770-6 Funtastic Frogs™ Math Volume 1

13

Use small and
medium frogs.
Record your work.

Name _____

A. Match the frogs.
Which circle has fewer frogs?

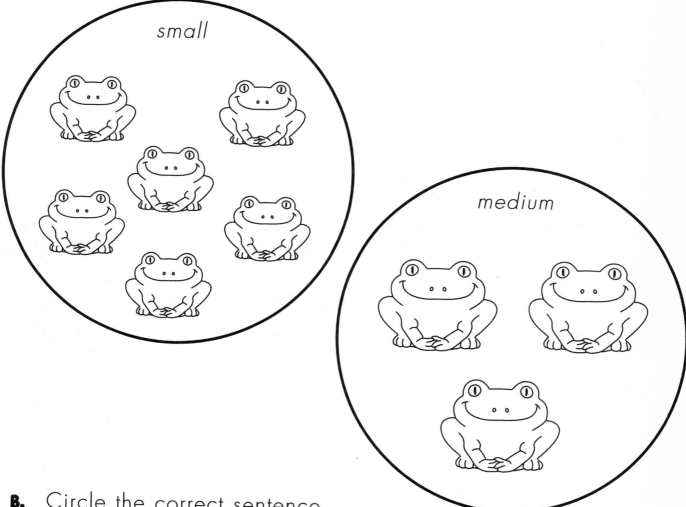

small

medium

B. Circle the correct sentence.

There are fewer small frogs.

There are fewer medium frogs.

ACTIVITY
14

Use small and
medium frogs.
Record your work.

Name _____

A. Match the frogs.
Compare the frogs in each circle.

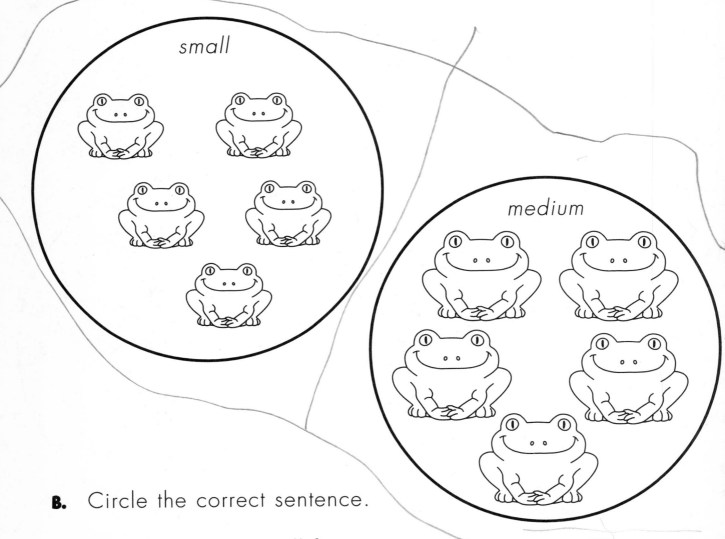

small

medium

B. Circle the correct sentence.

There are more small frogs.

There are more medium frogs.

The number of frogs in each circle is the same.

ACTIVITY 15

Use a bag of frogs.
Record your work.

Name _____

Look at the frogs in the bag.

A. Make a guess.

There are more ___snail___ frogs.

There are fewer ___medium___ frogs.

B. Open the bag.
Count the colors.

C. Fill in the sentences.

There are more _____ frogs.

There are fewer _____ frogs.

How well did you guess? ___same___

0-7424-2770-6 Funtastic Frogs™ Math Volume 1

ACTIVITY 16

Use small and medium frogs.
Record your work.

Name _____

Use the rules to sort the frogs.

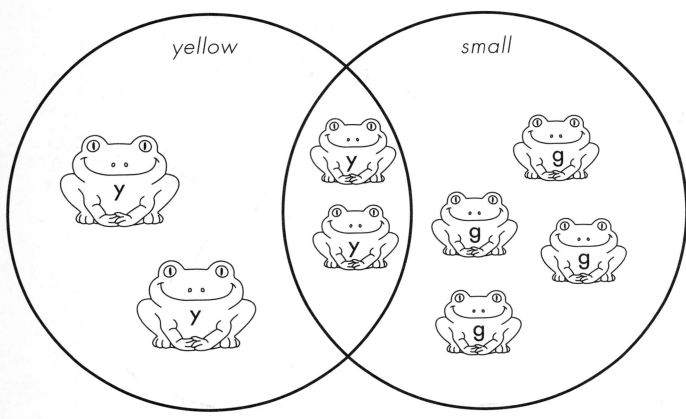

yellow   small

Which frogs belong in **both** circles?_____

ACTIVITY 17

Use small and
medium frogs.
Record your work.

Name _____

Use the rules to sort the frogs.

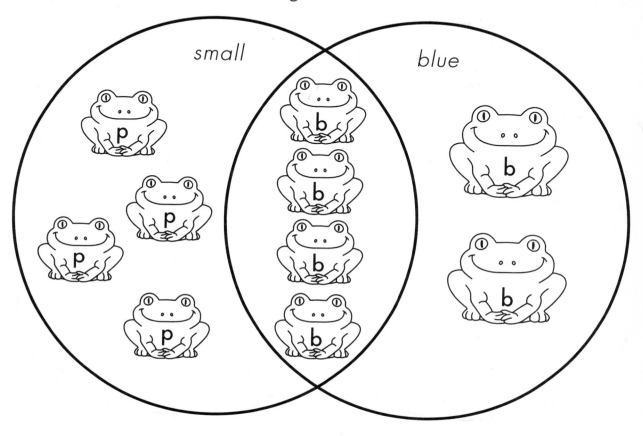

small   *blue*

Which frogs belong in **both** circles?_____

Sort by size and color

Use 3 small orange, 3 small red,
and 4 medium orange frogs
Record your work.

Name _____

Use the rules.
Put the frogs in the circles.
Draw a colored circle to show where each frog belongs.

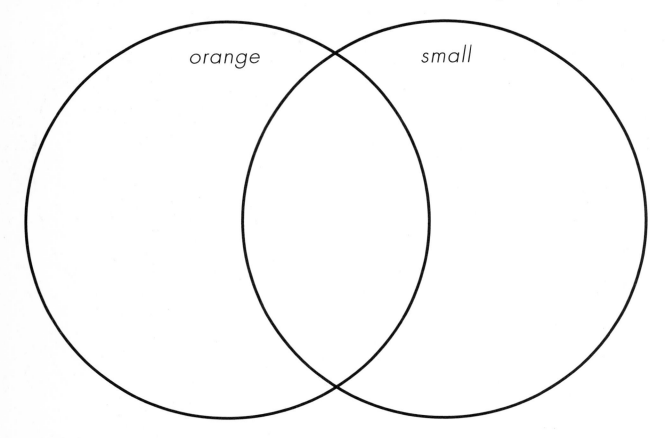

orange   small

Which frogs belong in **both** circles?_____

Name _____

Use 5 small green, 2 small purple,
and 2 medium green frogs.
Record your work.

Use the rules.
Put the frogs in the circles.
Draw a colored circle to show where each frog belongs.

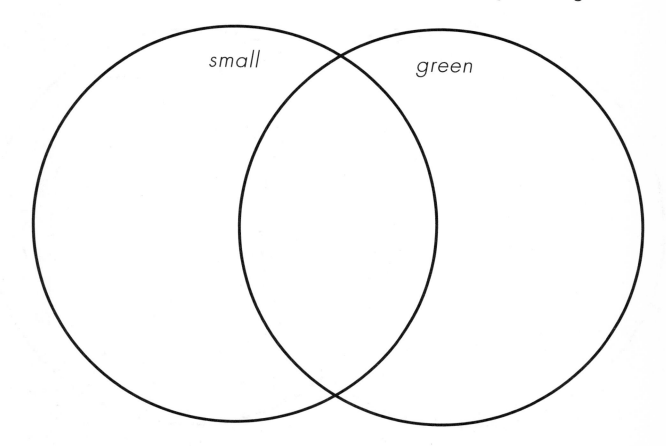

small

green

Which frogs belong in **both** circles?_____

Sort by size and color

ACTIVITY 20

Use 1 small green, 2 small purple,
1 small yellow, and 2 medium purple frogs.
Record your work.

Name _____

Write your own sorting rule for each circle.
Put frogs in the circles.
Draw a colored circle to show where each frog belongs.

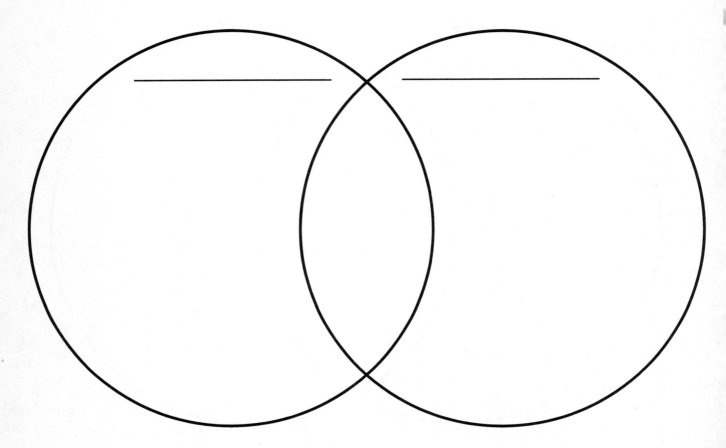

_____   _____

Which frogs belong in **both** circles?_____

The Match Game

READY

You need 3 small, 3 medium, and 3 large frogs in 3 different colors. Two of your colors must be the same as the other player's colors. One of your colors must be different from the other player's colors.

SET

Put the game board in front of you. Decide who goes first. The first player puts a frog on any square.

PLAY

Take turns putting frogs on the game board. The frog that you put down must match the color or size of another frog next to it, above it, or below it. If you cannot make a play, your turn is over. The last player to put down a frog wins the game.

PLAY AGAIN

Each player uses small, medium, and large frogs in two colors. The players use different colors. Take turns putting frogs on the game board. Each frog must be **different** in size or color from the frog next to it, above it, or below it. If you cannot make a play, your turn is over. The last player to put a frog on the board is the winner.

PLAY THE GAME BY YOURSELF

Use small, medium, and large frogs in 3 different colors. Place one frog at a time on the game board. Each frog must be different in size or color from the frog next to it, above it, or below it.

Name _____

The Match Game

FUNtastic FROGS™

Counting & Numbers

Unit II

Teacher's Notes for This Unit

In Unit II, *Counting & Numbers,* children use the frog counters to:
- count from one to twenty using one-to-one correspondence
- understand number concepts from one through twenty
- identify how many in a set of objects
- connect number words and numerals and the quantities they represent
- connect the size of cardinal numbers and the counting sequence
- act out the meaning of addition
- count-on to add one
- combine numbers
- compare two numbers to determine which is *more, less,* and the *same*
- order and compare numbers
- learn the vocabulary for ordering and comparing numbers

The activities in this unit are designed to teach number concepts using concrete objects. All the activities support current mathematics standards.

As children engage in these number activities, they will develop basic counting skills using the frog counters. They will recognize how many frogs are in a set or group. They will connect number words, the quantities they represent, and the numerals to the groups of frogs shown in the activities. They will make connections between the size of the numbers and the counting sequence. Finally, they will develop the ability to mentally visualize numbers.

Contents
This unit contains 20 activities divided into sections. Each section contains similar activities, giving the children the opportunity to practice and use each skill. Two counting workmats are included. These workmats may be utilized in multiple ways to allow children to apply what they have learned about counting and comparing numbers. You may use the 2 workmats included at the end of this unit to reinforce number activities, as the basis for making up story problems to solve, or to introduce the language used to identify location.

Math Skills and Understandings	**Related Activities**
Count from one to twenty using one-to-one correspondence	Activities 1–20
Understand number concepts through twenty	Activities 1–20
Connect number words, numerals, and the quantities they represent	Activities 1–20
Count-on to add one	Activities 1–5
Combine numbers to add	Activities 6–16
Compare two numbers to determine which is *more*, which is *less*, which is the *same*, and which is *in between*	Activities 16–20
Order and compare numbers	Activities 16–20
Learn the vocabulary for ordering and comparing numbers	Activities 16–20

Suggestions for Classroom Use

Encourage children to share their thinking with the whole class. Talking about their thinking and discoveries helps them clarify their thoughts and allows others to hear how they might solve the same problem a different way. Talking about how they solve problems helps children make mathematical connections and deepens their understanding.

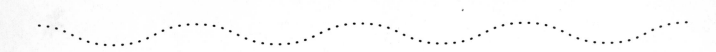

Materials

You may wish to make an overhead transparency of the first activity page in each section as an introduction to the activities that follow.

For each child, pair of children, or group, you will need:
- pencils
- crayons or colored markers to match the colors of the frogs
- a tub of frogs in three sizes and six colors
- an activity sheet for each child or pair of children

If children are not able to record by writing numbers and coloring, make copies of pages 44 and 45. The children can color and cut out the frogs, then paste or glue them in place to record.

Introducing the Activities
Encourage the children to compare the frogs and tell how they are alike and how they are different. Ask them to describe the sizes and the different weights. Ask questions to probe their thinking such as: *Can you show me five frogs? Can you show me five another way? Can you tell me how many green frogs you have? Do you have more green frogs or blue frogs?*

When you introduce the activities in a section, lead the children through the first activity in that section. Discuss the directions and how to record their work. After you have completed placing the frogs, point to the frogs and have the students count the numbers with you aloud. When reviewing the activity as a group, encourage the children to talk about their discoveries.

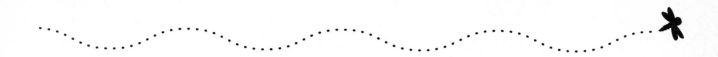

Mathematical Content by Section

Activities 1–5: Counting from one to ten. Children place the frogs on different objects and use one-to-one correspondence to count from one through ten. In this way, children experience composing the number tactilely and they gain a visual picture of what the number looks like. The *DO SOME MORE* option invites children to combine the two groups of frogs to find how many in all. While this section is not intended for addition instruction, this informal experience will further develop children's number sense, preparing them for more formal addition instruction at a later time.

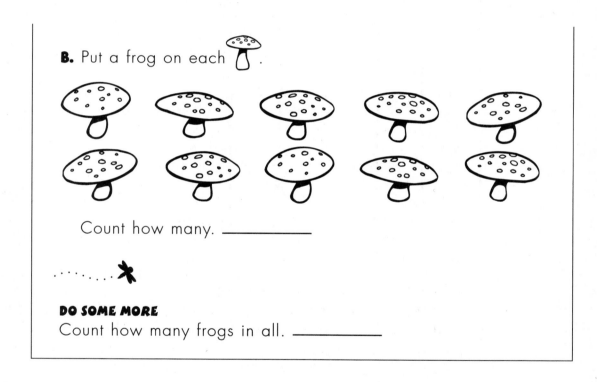

B. Put a frog on each 🍄 .

Count how many. _____

DO SOME MORE
Count how many frogs in all. _____

Activities 6–15: Counting from 11 to 20. The counting experiences in the first activities are reinforced as those numbers are used to compose numbers through 20. Children must recognize the numeral and place the corresponding number of frogs on each object. Informal addition experiences are provided as they combine the two groups on the page to find how many in all. The computation strategy, counting-on by one, is informally introduced in *DO SOME MORE*.

Activities 16–20: Ordering and comparing numbers. Children put frogs in numerical order on the pages then compare the groups to find which shows *more*, which shows *less*, which numbers are the *same*, and which number is *in between*. Using the frogs to construct these relationships helps the child experience the meaning of the relationships. They tactilely experience the numbers as well as have visual clues to find the relationships. Children apply what they have learned in the section to find the mystery number in the last activity.

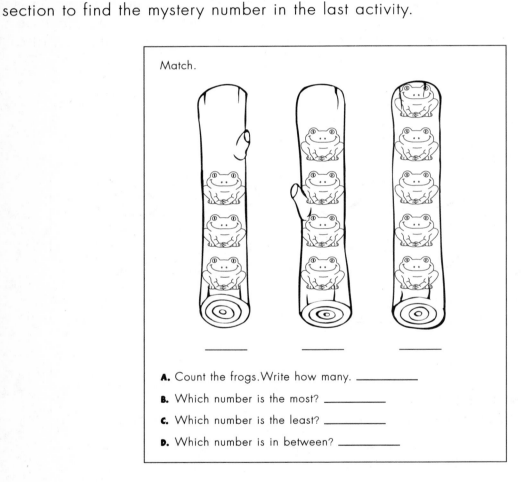

Match.

A. Count the frogs. Write how many. _____

B. Which number is the most? _____

C. Which number is the least? _____

D. Which number is in between? _____

Workmats: Use the frogs and these workmats to customize your instruction. You may wish to work with small groups of children to reinforce number concepts by directing them to place particular numbers or groups of frogs on the page to count. You can easily extend the learning on any activity page in this book. Children can place frogs on the page and write story problems for others to solve. The pages can be duplicated for children to color and make into a number book. They can draw or cut and paste different number concepts from 1 through 20 on the pages. You may also use these pages for assessment purposes.

Sample Solutions for This Unit

These are sample solutions. Additional solutions are possible for some activities.

Activity

1A. 1
1B. 2
DO SOME MORE 3

2A. 3
2B. 4
DO SOME MORE 7

3A. 5
3B. 6
DO SOME MORE 11

4A. 7
4B. 8
DO SOME MORE 15

5A. 9
5B. 10
DO SOME MORE 19

6A. 10
6B. 11

7A. 11
7B. 12

8A. 12
8B. 13

9A. 13
9B. 14

10A. 14
10B. 15

11A. 15
11B. 16

Activity

12A. 16
12B. 17

13A. 17
13B. 18

14A. 18
14B. 19

15A. 19
15B. 20

16A. Numbers of frogs from left: 1, 2, 3, 4, 5
16B. 5
16C. 1

17A. Numbers of frogs from left: 3, 4, 5
17B. 5
17C. 3
17D. 4

18A. Numbers of frogs from left: 3, 4, 5, 4, 3
18B. 4
18C 5

19A. Numbers of frogs from left: 3, 0.5, 6
19B. 4
19C. 6
19D. 0

20A. 9
20B. 14
DO SOME MORE Answers will vary.

Use large frogs.

Name _____

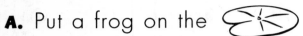

A. Put a frog on the .

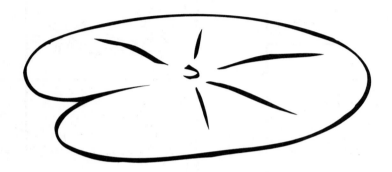

Count how many. _____

B. Put a frog on each ⬭ .

Count how many. _____

DO SOME MORE

Count how many frogs in all. _____

     0-7424-2770-6 *Funtastic Frogs™ Math Volume 1*

Name _____

Use medium frogs.

A. Put a frog on each .

Count how many. _____

B. Put a frog on each .

Count how many. _____

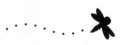

DO SOME MORE

Count how many frogs in all. _____

Use small frogs.

Name _____

A. Put a frog on each .

Count how many. _____

B. Put a frog on each 🍃.

Count how many. _____

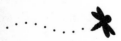

DO SOME MORE

Count how many frogs in all. _____

ACTIVITY 4

Use medium frogs.

Name _____

A. Put a frog on each  .

Count how many. _____

B. Put a frog on each ⬭ .

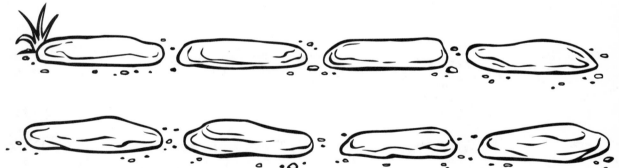

Count how many. _____

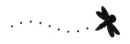

DO SOME MORE

Count how many frogs in all.

Name _____

Use small frogs.

A. Put a frog on each .

Count how many. _____

B. Put a frog on each .

Count how many. _____

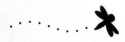

DO SOME MORE
Count how many frogs in all.

Name _____

A. Put frogs on each  to show the numbers.

Count how many frogs in all. _____

B. Put one more frog on one .

Count how many frogs in all.

Use small frogs.

Name _____

A. Put frogs on each  to show the numbers.

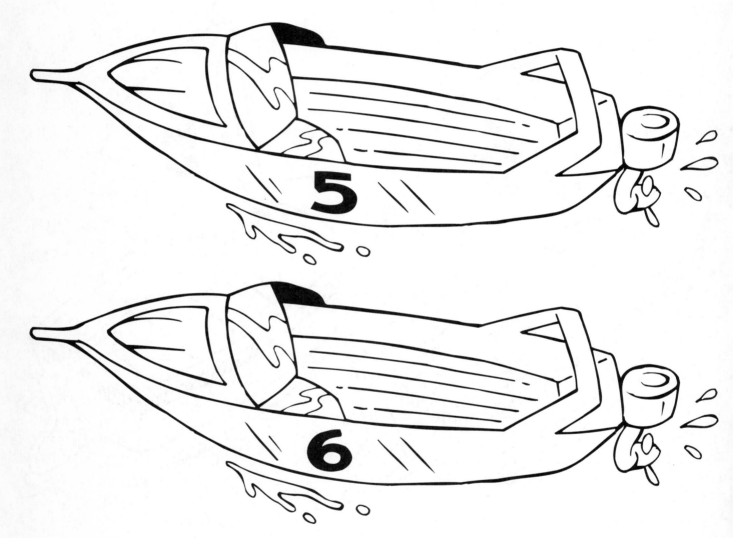

Count how many frogs in all. _____

B. Put one more frog on one  .

Count how many frogs in all. _____

Name _____

Use small frogs.

A. Put frogs on each  to show the numbers.

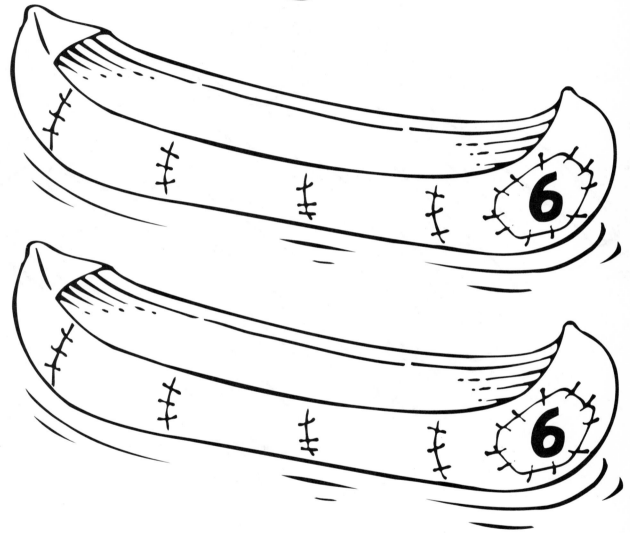

Count how many frogs in all. _____

B. Put one more frog on one  .

Count how many frogs in all.

Name _____

ACTIVITY 9

Use small frogs.

A. Put frogs on each 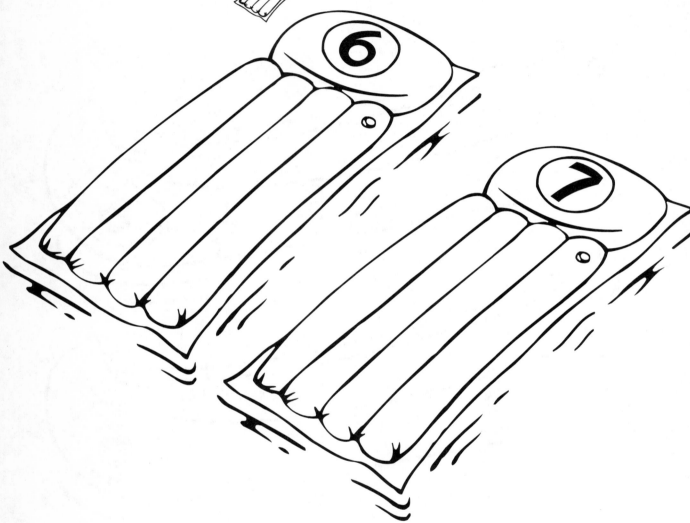 to show the numbers.

6

7

Count how many frogs in all. _____

B. Put one more frog on one  .

Count how many frogs in all. _____

Use small frogs.

Name _____

A. Put frogs on each to show the numbers.

Count how many frogs in all. _____

B. Put one more frog on one .

Count how many frogs in all. _____

Use small frogs.

Name _____

A. Put frogs on each  to show the numbers.

Count how many frogs in all. _____

B. Put one more frog on one  .

Count how many frogs in all. _____

Use small frogs.

Name _____

A. Put frogs on each  to show the numbers.

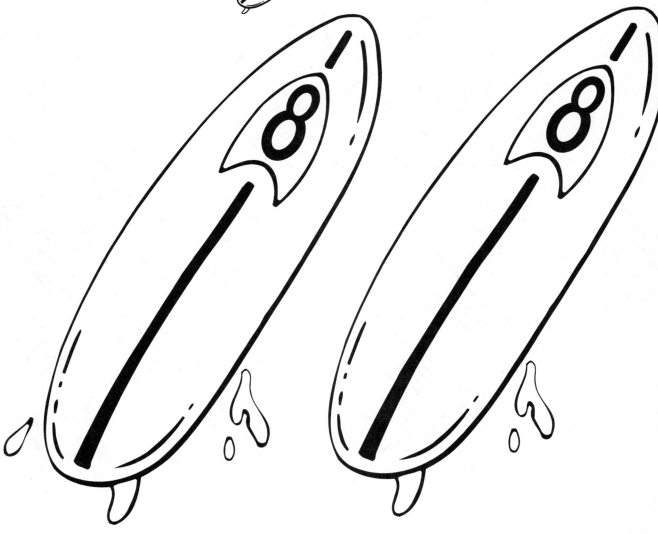

Count how many frogs in all. _____

B. Put one more frog on one .

Count how many frogs in all. _____

     0-7424-2770-6 *Funtastic Frogs™ Math Volume 1*

Name _____

Use small frogs.

A. Put frogs on each 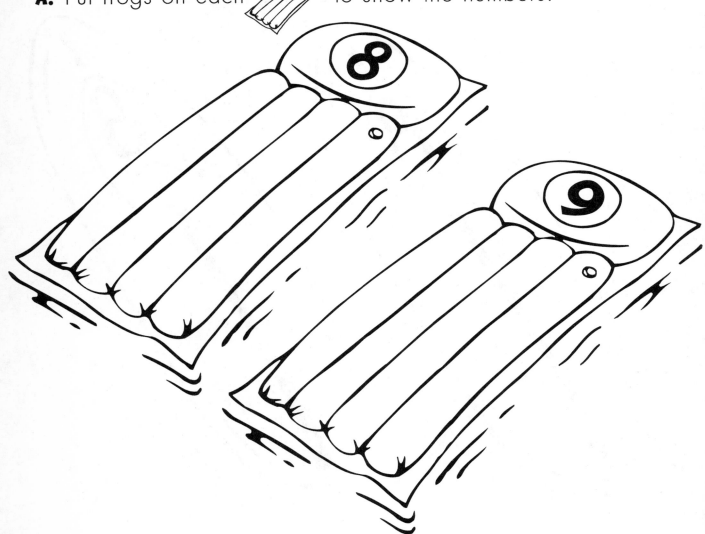 to show the numbers.

Count how many frogs in all. _____

B. Put one more frog on one  .

Count how many frogs in all. _____

Use small frogs.

Name _____

A. Put frogs on each to show the numbers.

Count how many frogs in all. _____

B. Put one more frog on one .

Count how many frogs in all. _____

0-7424-2770-6 Funtastic Frogs™ Math Volume 1

ACTIVITY 15

Use small frogs.

A. Put frogs in each  to show the numbers.

Count how many frogs in all. _____

B. Put one more frog in one .

Count how many frogs in all. _____

Name _____

Use small frogs.

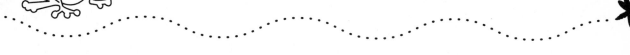

Match.

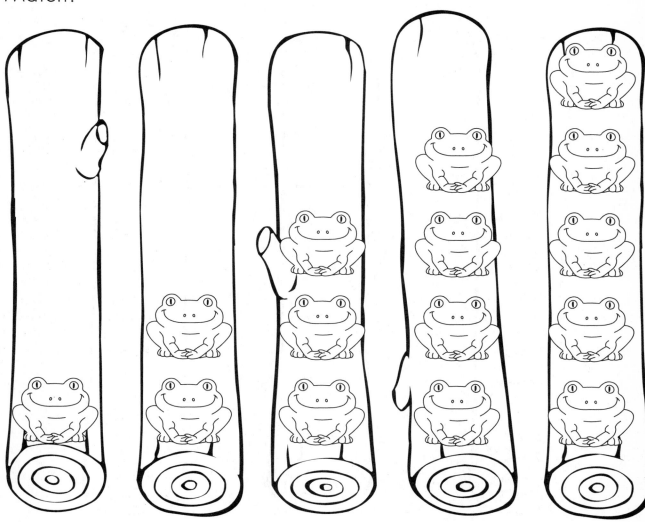

____ ____ ____ ____ ____

A. Count the frogs. Write how many.

B. Which number is the most? _____

C. Which number is the least? _____

61   0-7424-2770-6 Funtastic Frogs™ Math Volume 1

Name _____

Use small frogs.

Match.

_____   _____   _____

A. Count the frogs. Write how many.

B. Which number is the most? _____

C. Which number is the least? _____

D. Which number is in between? _____

Name _____

Use small frogs.
Match the clues.
Write the number of frogs.

Example:
There are more than 4 frogs.
There are less than 6 frogs.

How many frogs? 5

A. There are more than 8 frogs.
There are less than 10 frogs.

How many frogs? _____

B. There are more than 13 frogs.
There are less than 15 frogs.

How many frogs? _____

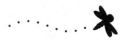

DO SOME MORE
Make your own clues.
Let someone find how many frogs.

WORKMAT 1

Name _____

FUNtastic FROGS™

Balancing Numbers

Unit III

Teacher's Notes for This Unit

In Unit III, *Balancing Numbers,* children use the frog counters in activities to:
* represent numerical situations using concrete objects
* work with variables, numbers, and equations in an informal way
* work with the order property of addition in an informal way
* develop number sense
* represent the same number in different ways
* understand the meaning of addition
* find sums through 15
* show equal sums using different numbers
* compare numbers to find which is *more than*, *less than*, and *the same as*
* use appropriate representations of mathematical situations
* solve problems using logical reasoning

The activities in this unit are designed to teach different ways of representing equal values. All the activities support current mathematics standards.

As children engage in these activities, they will model equal values using the frog counters and a simple balance. They will develop the understanding that equal values can be shown in different ways and that the order of numbers does not affect the sum. The activities will help children think flexibly about numbers and will help build a foundation for understanding variables and equations when they encounter formal algebra instruction in later years.

Contents
This unit contains 22 activities divided into four sections: finding equal values, comparing number relationships to find which is *more than*, comparing number relationships to find which is *less than*, and comparing number relationships to find which is *more than*, *less than*, and *the same as*. The activities in each section are similar, giving the children the opportunity to practice and use each skill.

Math Skills and Understandings	Related Activities
Represent numbers using concrete objects	Activities 1–22
Work with variables, numbers, and equations in an informal way	Activities 1–22
Represent numbers in different ways	Activities 1–22
Understand the meaning of addition	Activities 1–22
Find sums through 15	Activities 1–22
Find equal sums using different numbers	Activities 1–22
Compare values to find which is *more than*, *less than*, and *the same as*	Activities 10–22
Use appropriate representations of mathematical situations	Activities 1–22
Use logic and reasoning to solve problems	Activities 1–22

Suggestions for Classroom Use

Encourage children to share their thinking with the whole class. When working together, they often discover multiple ways to solve a problem. Talking about their thinking and discoveries helps them clarify their thoughts and allows others to hear how they might solve the same problem a different way. Talking about how they solve problems helps children make mathematical connections and deepens their understanding. Class discussions encourage the type of thinking required for reasoning and problem solving.

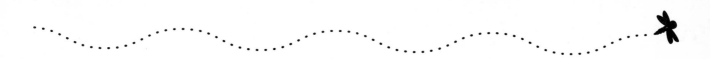

Materials

You may wish to make an overhead transparency of the first activity page in each section as an introduction to the activities that follow.

For each child, pair of children, or group you will need:
- pencils
- crayons or colored markers to match the colors of the frogs
- a tub of frogs in three sizes and six colors
- an activity sheet for each child or pair of children
- a balance for the whole class or each group

Introducing the Activities

Allow groups to explore using the frogs with the balance. You can use this exploration period to introduce vocabulary that will be used throughout the unit, such as *balance*, *left*, *right*, and *value*.

When you introduce each section, lead the children through the first activity in that section. Discuss the directions and how to record their work. After you have completed placing the frogs, point to the frogs and have the students count the values with you aloud.

After the children complete the activities, have them talk about how they showed the numbers. Help them extend their thinking by asking such questions as: *Which values were easiest to show? Which were hardest? How can you be sure that the frogs you used on the balance were correct?* After children have worked through the first section, ask more probing questions such as: *What do you notice about the number sentences? Did you find any patterns? What number can be made using the most number combinations?* Encourage children who finish early to look for number relationships for numbers through 20 and beyond.

Mathematical Content by Section

Activities 1–10: Find equal values. To introduce Activities 1–5, tell the children that each small frog has a value of 1. Show five small frogs and ask children to find the total value. Repeat the activity several times using different numbers of small frogs. Next tell the children that each medium frog has a value of 2. Show five medium frogs and ask children to find the total value. Repeat this several times, using different numbers of medium frogs.

Show a combination of small and medium frogs and ask children to find the total value. Ask different children to come up and explain how to find the total. If necessary, show the children how to count-on by one or two for each frog to find the total value.

Use the frog counters and the balance to demonstrate a number sentence that shows the same value on each side. Put four small frogs on the left side of the balance. Ask: *How many small frogs do I need on the other side to balance? Can you show me the same value using the medium frogs?* As volunteers place medium frogs on the right side to balance, have them explain their reasoning. Point out that there is more than one way to balance the value on the left. Show the children how to write the balanced number sentences that have been demonstrated, using an equal sign to represent the middle of the balance.

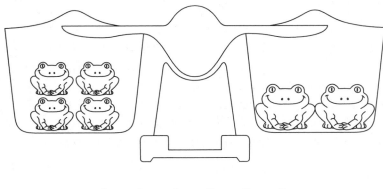

$$1 + 1 + 1 + 1 = 2 + 2$$

To introduce Activity 6, show a large frog and explain that it has a value of 4. Ask children to find the total value of one small, one medium, and one large frog (7). Then make different combinations of frogs for them to solve. Demonstrate using the balance to solve problems with the three sizes of frogs before assigning Activities 6–10.

Activities 11–15: Comparing number relationships to find which is *more than*.
Children apply what they have learned about writing balanced number sentences to find which side of the balance has a higher value, or *more than*. To introduce the activities, tell the children that each large frog has a value of 4. Place three large frogs on the left side of the balance and one large frog on the right. Ask the children to tell, by looking at the balance, which side has more. Have them explain their reasoning, making sure they note the relationship between the position of the balance and the value of the numbers—with the larger number value pushing down its side of the balance. Repeat, using different frogs and number values. Model showing the relationship, using the number sentence on page 87.

more than

B. Fill in the number sentence.

_____ is more than _____

Activities 16–20: Comparing number relationships to find which is *less than*.
Children apply what they have learned about comparing numbers to find which side of the balance has *less*. To introduce the activities, tell the children that each small frog has a value of 1. Place two small frogs on the left side of the balance and one large frog on the right. Ask the children to tell, by looking at the balance, which side has less. Have children explain their reasoning, making sure they note the relationship between the position of the balance (with the higher number value "weighing" more) and the value of the numbers. Repeat, using different frogs and number values. Model how children can show the relationship, using the number sentence on page 92.

Activities 21–22: Comparing number relationships to find which is *more than*, *less than*, and *the same as*. Introduce these activities by asking children to imagine that the frogs on each side are placed on the balance. The children will then apply what they have learned to determine what kind of number relationship is shown on the balance.

Sample Solutions for This Unit

These are sample solutions. Additional solutions are possible for some activities.

Activity

1A. 4 or 1+1+1+1
1B. 1+1+1+1=2+2
EXPLORE MORE 1+1+1+1=1+1+2

2A. 2+2+2
2B. 2+2+2=1+1+1+1+1+1
EXPLORE MORE 2+2+2=1+1+1+1+2

3A. 2+2+1+1+1
3A. 2+2+1+1+1=2+2+2+1
EXPLORE MORE 2+2+1+1+1=2+1+1+1+1+1

4A. 2+2+2+2
4B. 2+2+2+2=2+2+2+1+1
EXPLORE MORE 2+2+2+2=2+2+1+1+1+1

5A. 2+2+2+2+1
5B. 2+2+2+2+1=2+2+2+1+1+1
EXPLORE MORE 2+2+2+2+1=2+2+1+1+1+1+1

6A. 2+2+2+2+2
6B. 2+2+2+2+2=2+2+2+1+1+1+1
EXPLORE MORE 2+2+2+2+2=2+2+1+1+1+1+1+1

7A. 6
7B. 6=3+3
EXPLORE MORE 6=6

8A. 3+3+3
8B. 3+3+3=3+6
EXPLORE MORE 3+3+3=6+3

9A. 12
9B. 12=6+6
EXPLORE MORE 12=3+3+6

10A. 6+6+3
10B. 6+6+3=3+12
EXPLORE MOREE 6+6+3=6+3+6

11A. 8
11B. 8 is more than 2+2

Activity

12A. 2+8
12B. 2+8 is more than 2+2+2
EXPLORE MORE 2+8 is more than 8

13A. 4+8
13B. 4+8 is more than 2+8
EXPLORE MORE 4+8 is more than 4+4

14A. 2+4+4
14B. 2+4+4 is more than 2+4
EXPLORE MORE 2+4+4 is more than 2+2+4

15A. 2+2+2+2+2
15B. 2+2+2+2+2 is more than 8+2
EXPLORE MORE 2+2+2+2+2 is more than 2+2+4

16A. 4
16B. 8
16C. 4 is less than 8
EXPLORE MORE 4 is less than 2+4

17A. 8
17B. 4
17C. 4 is less than 8
EXPLORE MORE 2+4 is less than 8

18A. 2+8
18B. 2+4
18C. 2+4 is less than 2+8
EXPLORE MORE 2+2+4 is less than 10

19A. 2+4+8
19B. 4+8
19C. 4+8 is less than 2+4+8
EXPLORE MORE 2+8 is less than 2+4+8

20A. 2+2+2+2+2
20B. 4
20C. 4 is less than 2+2+2+2+2
EXPLORE MORE 8 is less than 2+2+2+2+2

21A. 2+2
21B. 4
21C. 2+2 is the same as 4

22A. 8+2
22B. 4+4
22C. 2+8 is more than 4+4

0-7424-2770-6 Funtastic Frogs™ Math Volume 1

This page may be used to create your own activity sheets.

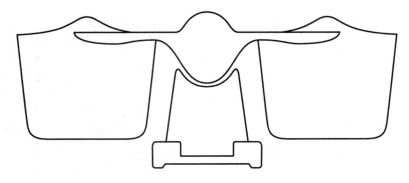

_____ **is the same as** _____

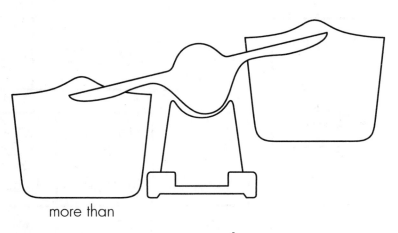

more than

_____ **is more than** _____

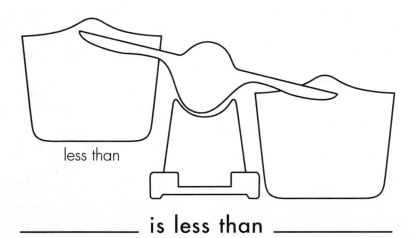

less than

_____ **is less than** _____

Name _____

Use small and medium frogs.
Record you work.

Each small frog has a value of 1.

Each medium frog has a value of 2.

A. What is the value of the frogs
on the left side of the balance? ___4___

Put medium frogs on the right side to balance.
The right side must have the same value as the left side.

B. Write a balanced number sentence.

1 + 1 + 1 + 1 = ___4___

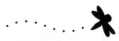

EXPLORE MORE
Find another way to balance the number sentence.

ACTIVITY 2

Name _____

Use small and medium frogs.
Record your work.

Each small frog has a value of 1.

Each medium frog has a value of 2.

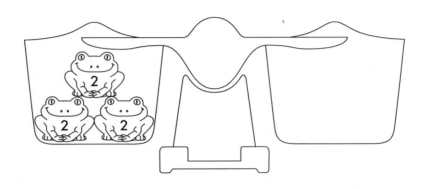

A. What is the value of the frogs
on the left side of the balance? _____

Put small frogs on the right side to balance.
The right side must have the same value as the left side.

B. Write a balanced number sentence.

2 + 2 + 2 = _____

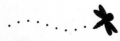

EXPLORE MORE
Find another way to balance the number sentence.

Use small and medium frogs.
Record your work.

Name _____

Each small frog has a value of 1.

Each medium frog has a value of 2.

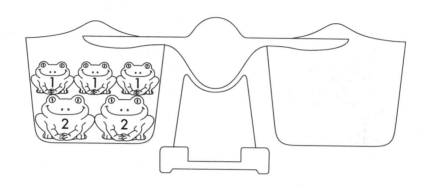

A. What is the value of the frogs
on the left side of the balance? _____

Put frogs on the right side to balance.
The right side must have the same value as the left side.

B. Write a balanced number sentence.

2 + 2 + 1 + 1 + 1 = _____

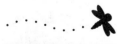

EXPLORE MORE
Find another way to balance the number sentence.

Name _____

Use small and medium frogs.
Record your work.

Each small frog has a value of 1.

Each medium frog has a value of 2.

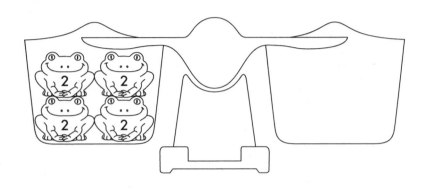

A. What is the value of the frogs
on the left side of the balance? _____

Put frogs on the right side to balance.
The right side must have the same value as the left side.

B. Write a balanced number sentence.

2 + 2 + 2 + 2 = _____

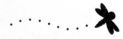

EXPLORE MORE

Find another way to balance the number sentence.

Use small and medium frogs.
Record your work.

Name _____

Each small frog has a value of 1.

Each medium frog has a value of 2.

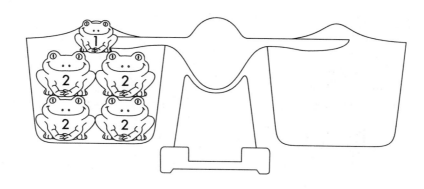

A. What is the value of the frogs
on the left side of the balance? _____

Put frogs on the right side to balance.
The right side must have the same value as the left side.

B. Write a balanced number sentence.

2 + 2 + 2 + 2 + 1 = _____

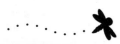

EXPLORE MORE

Find another way to balance the number sentence.

Name _____

Use small, medium, and large frogs.
Record your work.

Each small frog has a value of 1.

Each medium frog has a value of 2.

Each large frog has a value of 4.

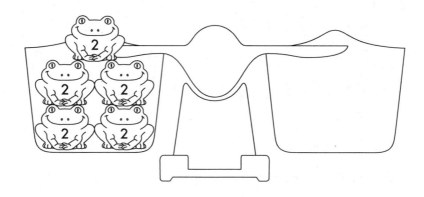

A. What is the value of the frogs
on the left side of the balance? _____

Put frogs on the right side to balance.
The right side must have the same value as the left side.

B. Write a balanced number sentence.

2 + 2 + 2 + 2 + 2 = _____

EXPLORE MORE
Find another way to balance the number sentence.

Use small and medium frogs.
Record your work.

Name _____

Each small frog has a value of 3.

Each medium frog has a value of 6.

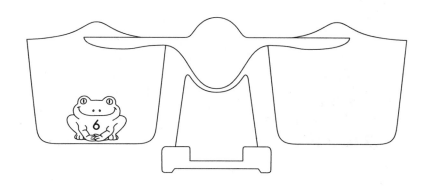

A. What is the value of the frog
on the left side of the balance? _____

Put frogs on the right side to balance.
The right side must have the same value as the left side.

B. Write a balanced number sentence.

6 = _____

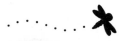

EXPLORE MORE
Find another way to balance the number sentence.

Use small and medium frogs.
Record your work.

Name _____

Each small frog has a value of 3.

Each medium frog has a value of 6.

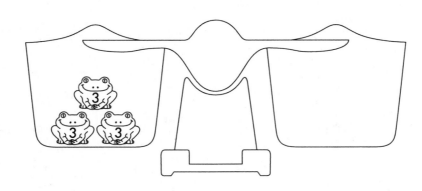

A. What is the value of the frogs
on the left side of the balance? _____

Put frogs on the right side to balance.
The right side must have the same value as the left side.

B. Write a balanced number sentence.

3 + 3 + 3 = _____

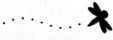

EXPLORE MORE
Find another way to balance the number sentence.

Name _____

Use small, medium, and large frogs.
Record your work.

Each small frog has a value of 3.

Each medium frog has a value of 6.

Each large frog has a value of 12.

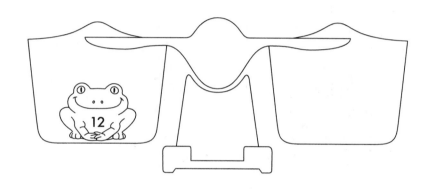

A. What is the value of the frog
on the left side of the balance? _____

Put frogs on the right side to balance.
The right side must have the same value as the left side.

B. Write a balanced number sentence.

12 = _____

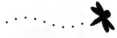

EXPLORE MORE
Find another way to balance the number sentence.

Name _____

Use small, medium, and large frogs.
Record your work.

Each small frog has a value of 3.

Each medium frog has a value of 6.

Each large frog has a value of 12.

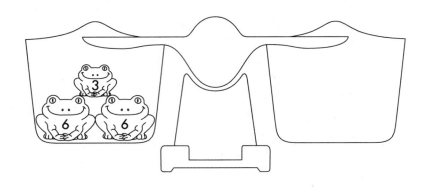

A. What is the value of the frogs
on the left side of the balance? _____

Put frogs on the right side to balance.
The right side must have the same value as the left side.

B. Write a balanced number sentence.

6 + 6 + 3 = _____

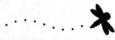

EXPLORE MORE
Find another way to balance the number sentence.

Name _____

Use small, medium, and large frogs.
Record your work.

Each small frog has a value of 2.

Each medium frog has a value of 4.

Each large frog has a value of 8.

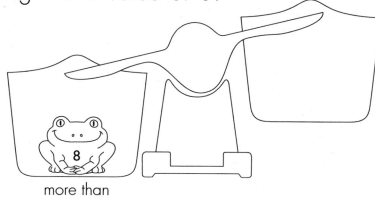

more than

A. What is the value of the frog
on the left side of the balance? _____

Put 2 small frogs on the right side of the balance
to make the picture true.

more than

B. Fill in the number sentence.

_____ is more than _____

Name _____

Use small, medium, and large frogs.
Record your work.

Each small frog has a value of 2.

Each medium frog has a value of 4.

Each large frog has a value of 8.

more than

A. What is the value of the frogs
on the left side of the balance? _____

Put frogs on the right side of the balance
to make the picture true.

B. Fill in the number sentence.

_____ is more than _____

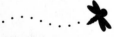

EXPLORE MORE
Find another way to make the picture true.
Fill in the number sentence.

_____ is more than _____

ACTIVITY 13

Use small, medium, and large frogs.
Record your work.

Name _____

Each small frog has a value of 2.

Each medium frog has a value of 4.

Each large frog has a value of 8.

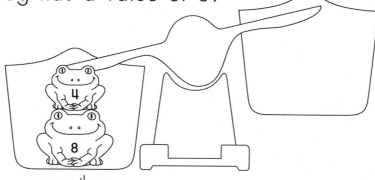

more than

A. What is the value of the frogs
on the left side of the balance? _____

Put frogs on the right side of the balance
to make the picture true.

B. Fill in the number sentence.

_____ is more than _____

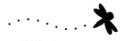

EXPLORE MORE

Find another way to make the picture true.
Fill in the number sentence.

_____ is more than _____

       0-7424-2770-6 Funtastic Frogs™ Math Volume 1

Use small, medium, and large frogs.
Record your work.

Name _____

Each small frog has a value of 2.

Each medium frog has a value of 4.

Each large frog has a value of 8.

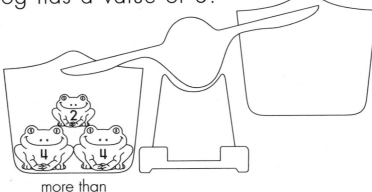

more than

A. What is the value of the frogs
on the left side of the balance? _____

Put frogs on the right side of the balance
to make the picture true.

B. Fill in the number sentence.

_____ is more than _____

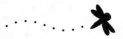

EXPLORE MORE

Find another way to make the picture true.
Fill in the number sentence.

_____ is more than _____

Use small, medium, and large frogs.
Record your work.

Name _____

Each small frog has a value of 2.

Each medium frog has a value of 4.

Each large frog has a value of 8.

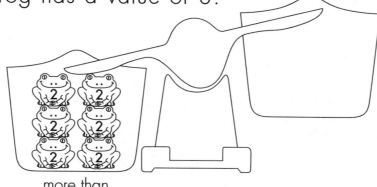

more than

A. What is the value of the frogs
on the left side of the balance? _____

Put frogs on the right side of the balance
to make the picture true.

B. Fill in the number sentence.

_____ is more than _____

EXPLORE MORE
Find another way to make the picture true.
Fill in the number sentence.

_____ is more than _____

Name _____

Use small, medium, and large frogs.
Record your work.

Each small frog has a value of 2.

Each medium frog has a value of 4.

Each large frog has a value of 8.

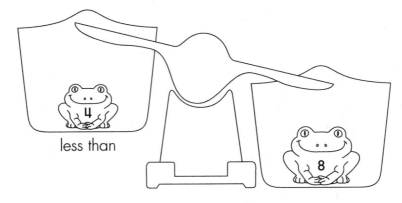

less than

A. What is the value of the frog
on the left side of the balance? _____

B. What is the value of the frog
on the right side of the balance? _____

C. Fill in the number sentence.

_____ is less than _____

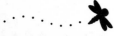

EXPLORE MORE
Find another way to make the picture true.
Fill in the number sentence.

_____ is less than _____

Name _____

Use small, medium, and large frogs.
Record your work.

Each small frog has a value of 2.

Each medium frog has a value of 4.

Each large frog has a value of 8.

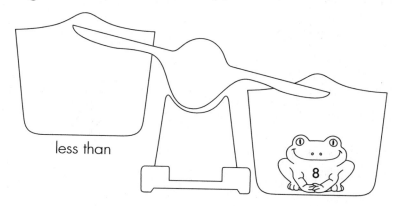

less than

8

A. What is the value of the frog
on the right side of the balance? _____

Put frogs on the left side to make the picture true.

B. What is the value of the frogs
on the left side of the balance? _____

C. Fill in the number sentence.

_____ is less than _____

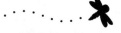

EXPLORE MORE
Find another way to make the picture true.
Fill in the number sentence.

_____ is less than _____

Use small, medium, and large frogs.
Record your work.

Name _____

Each small frog has a value of 2.

Each medium frog has a value of 4.

Each large frog has a value of 8.

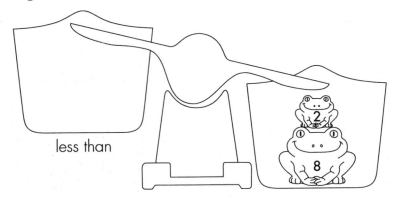

less than

A. What is the value of the frogs
on the right side of the balance? _____

Put frogs on the left side to make the picture true.

B. What is the value of the frogs
on the left side of the balance? _____

C. Fill in the number sentence.

_____ is less than _____

EXPLORE MORE

Find another way to make the picture true.
Fill in the number sentence.

_____ is less than _____

Name _____

Use small, medium, and large frogs.
Record your work.

Each small frog has a value of 2.

Each medium frog has a value of 4.

Each large frog has a value of 8.

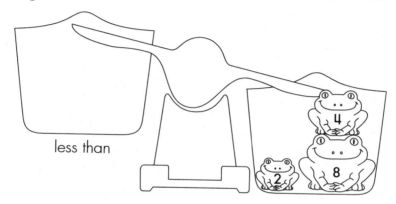

less than

A. What is the value of the frogs
on the right side of the balance? _____

Put frogs on the left side to make the picture true.

B. What is the value of the frogs
on the left side of the balance? _____

C. Fill in the number sentence.

_____ is less than _____

EXPLORE MORE
Find another way to make the picture true.
Fill in the number sentence.

_____ is less than _____

Name _____

Use small, medium, and large frogs.
Record your work.

Each small frog has a value of 2.

Each medium frog has a value of 4.

Each large frog has a value of 8.

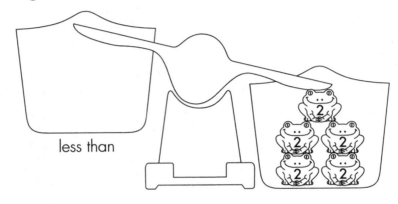

less than

A. What is the value of the frogs
on the right side of the balance? _____

Put frogs on the left side to make the picture true.

B. What is the value of the frogs
on the left side of the balance? _____

C. Fill in the number sentence.

_____ is less than _____

EXPLORE MORE
Find another way to make the picture true.
Fill in the number sentence.

_____ is less than _____

Name _____

Use small and medium frogs.
Record your work.

Each small frog has a value of 2.

Each medium frog has a value of 4.

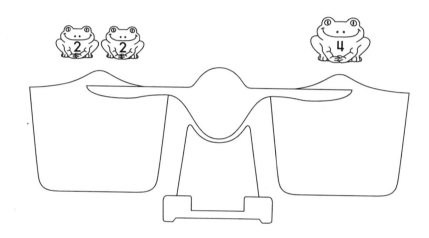

A. Find the value of the frogs on the left side. _____

B. Find the value of the frog on the right side. _____

C. Circle the correct sentence.
Use frogs and a balance to check your answer.

2 + 2 is more than 4

2 + 2 is the same as 4

2 + 2 is less than 4

Name _____

Use small, medium, and large frogs.

Each small frog has a value of 2.

Each medium frog has a value of 4.

Each large frog has a value of 8.

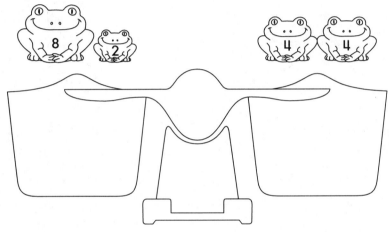

A. What is the value of the frogs
on the left side of the balance? _____

B. What is the value of the frogs
on the right side of the balance? _____

C. Circle the correct sentence.
Use frogs and a balance to check your answer.

2 + 8 is more than 4 + 4

2 + 8 is the same as 4 + 4

2 + 8 is less than 4 + 4

FUNtastic FROGS™

Measuring

Unit IV

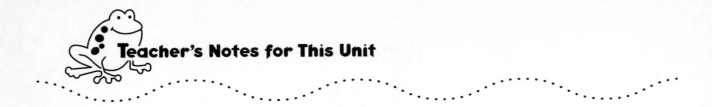

Teacher's Notes for This Unit

In Unit IV, *Measuring*, children use the frog counters to:
- understand and use vocabulary related to measurement
- recognize the attributes of length, weight, perimeter, and area
- estimate measurements
- measure length, weight, perimeter, and area using nonstandard units
- compare and order objects to find relationships
- develop referents for units of measure

The informal measurement activities in this unit are designed to teach the concepts of measurement and develop the process skills involved in measuring. All the activities support current mathematics standards.

As children engage in these measurement activities, they will make visual comparisons using concrete objects. They will use the frogs to measure and will connect the repeated physical action of measuring to the repeated unit of measure. They will develop an understanding of the concepts of length, weight, perimeter, and area. The act of measuring commonly used objects helps connect the activities to a child's real world.

Many activities involve estimation. Estimating, or guessing, is an important skill in measurement as it is in all mathematics. Children develop benchmarks for units of measure through repeated experiences in estimating and measuring.

Contents
This unit includes 20 activities divided into sections on length, weight, perimeter, and area. Each section features five similar activities, giving children the opportunity to use and practice each skill.

The unit also includes four investigations involving frogs and bullfrogs. These investigations allow children to apply what they have learned about measurement as they explore the physical characteristics of frogs.

Math Skills and Understandings

Understand and use vocabulary related to measurement

Estimate measurements

Recognize the attribute of length

Recognize the attribute of weight

Recognize the attribute of perimeter

Recognize the attribute of area

Measure with same-size nonstandard units

Make and use measurements in natural situations

Compare objects to find relationships

Develop referents for units through estimation

Use iteration to find length and area

Related Activities

Activities 1–20; Investigations 1–4

Activities 1–20; Investigations 1–4

Activities 1–5; Investigations 1–4

Activities 6–10

Activities 11–15; Investigation 1

Activities 16–20; Investigation 1

Activities 1–20; Investigations 1–4

Activities 1–20; Investigations 1–4

Activities 6–10

Activities 1–20; Investigations 1–4

Activities 1–5; 16–20; Investigations 1–4

Suggestions for Classroom Use

Encourage children to share their thinking with the whole class. Talking about their thinking and discoveries helps them clarify their thoughts and allows others to hear how they might solve the same problem a different way. Talking about how they solve problems helps children make mathematical connections and deepens their understanding.

Materials

You may wish to make an overhead transparency of the first activity page in each section as an introduction to the activities that follow.

For each child, pair of children, or group, you will need:
- pencils
- crayons or colored markers to match the colors of the frogs
- a tub of frogs in three sizes and six colors
- an activity sheet for each child or pair of children

Note that Activities 6–10 require a balance.

The Investigations will also require:
- scissors
- glue or paste
- string

Introducing the Activities

When you introduce a section of the unit, lead the children through the first activity in that section. Discuss the directions and how to record their work. Encourage the children to guess (estimate) before measuring. Point out that a guess does not have to be correct. Also, due to the nature of the frog counters, measurements will not be exact. For example, *a line about six frogs long* is an acceptable measurement. You may wish to model that language as you introduce the activities. When reviewing an activity as a group, encourage the children to talk about their discoveries. This will help them make connections and clarify their thinking.

Mathematical Content by Section

Activities 1–5: Measuring length using nonstandard units. Children develop a sense of length as they estimate then use same-size frog counters to measure a caterpillar, their pencils, scissors, and shoes. They refine their sense of length as they estimate and use same-size frogs to measure two different worms, their hands, thumbs, a book, their desks, and other common objects.

Activities 6–10: Measuring weight using nonstandard units. Children develop a sense of weight as they use a balance to compare different groups of frog counters. They develop an understanding of the terms *heavier* and *lighter* and learn that when both sides balance, the weights are *the same*. They use that knowledge to estimate then measure how many frogs will balance common classroom objects.

Activities 11–15: Measuring perimeter using nonstandard units. Children develop a sense of perimeter as they estimate then use same-size frog counters to measure the distances around the outsides of common shapes, frog's swimming pool, a log, a book, and their desks. They estimate and measure the perimeter of the same-size shapes using small, medium, and large frogs then discuss the different results.

Activities 16–20: Measuring area using nonstandard units. Children develop a sense of area as they estimate then use same-size frog counters to cover the surface area of two lily pads, a flower, a banana, two rafts, a house, and a bus.

Investigations 1–4: Measuring length, perimeter, and area using nonstandard units. Children use small frog counters to explore the physical attributes of a bullfrog by measuring its length, perimeter, and surface area. They make and use a frog ruler to measure common objects. They also explore how far some frogs can jump and speculate how far they could jump if they were a frog.

Sample Solutions for This Unit

These are sample solutions. The measurements given are approximate. Children may vary the way they place the frogs when measuring. Accept all reasonable answers.

Activity

1A. About 4 small frogs **1B.** About 2 small frogs
1C. About 6 small frogs
EXPLORE MORE Using medium frogs: ≈4 frogs; ≈2 frogs; ≈4 frogs. Using large frogs: ≈3 frogs, ≈2 frogs, ≈4 frogs.

2 Answers will vary.

3 Worm A is the longer worm. **3A.** About 8 small
3B. About 6 small
EXPLORE MORE Using medium frogs: ≈7 frogs; ≈5 frogs. Using large frogs: ≈6 frogs; ≈4 frogs

4 Answers will vary. **5** Answers will vary.

6A. Large frog **6B.** Medium frog
EXPLORE MORE 2 small frogs =1 medium frog

7A. Heavier group: 2 small frogs
7B. Lighter group: 1 small frog
EXPLORE MORE 3 small frogs balance 3 small frogs.

8A. Heavier group: 3 medium frogs
8B. Lighter group: 3 medium frogs

9A. Heavier group: 2 large frogs
9B. Lighter group: 2 large frogs
EXPLORE MORE 3 small frogs balance 3 small frogs.

10 Answers will vary.

11A. About 14 small **11B.** About 16 small
TALK ABOUT IT The numbers differ because the sizes of the pictures differ.

12A. About 14 medium **12B.** About 15 medium
TALK ABOUT IT The numbers differ because the sizes of the objects differ.

13A. About 11 large **13B.** Answers will vary.

14A. About 20 small **14B.** About 18 medium
14C. About 17 large
TALK ABOUT IT The numbers differ because the sizes of the base of the frogs differ.

Activity

15A. Answers will vary. **15B.** Answers will vary.
TALK ABOUT IT The numbers differ because the sizes of the two frogs differ.

16A. About 6 small **16B.** About 13 small
TALK ABOUT IT The numbers differ because the sizes of the lily pads differ.

17A. About 7 medium **17B.** About 6 medium
EXPLORE MORE About 10 small frogs; about 8 small frogs. The numbers differ because the sizes of the frogs differ.

18A. About 8 large **18B.** About 12 large
EXPLORE MORE About 15 small frogs; about 24 small frogs; about 10 medium frogs; about 14 medium frogs. The numbers differ because the sizes of the frogs differ. The measurements are not exact.

19A. About 32 small **19B.** About 28 medium
19C. About 18 large
TALK ABOUT IT The numbers differ because the sizes of the frogs differ.

20A. About 28 small **20B.** About 20 medium
20C. About 19 large
TALK ABOUT IT The numbers differ because the sizes of the frogs differ.

INVESTIGATION 1A. About 9 small
1B. About 32 small **1C.** About 48 small

INVESTIGATION 2 The ruler is about six inches long. Children will find objects about six inches long such as a stapler or a calculator.

INVESTIGATION 3A. Objects about six inches long such as sissors or a flashcard.
3B. Objects about four inches long such as a crayon. **3C.** Objects about two inches long such as a large paper clip.

INVESTIGATION 4 Answers will vary.

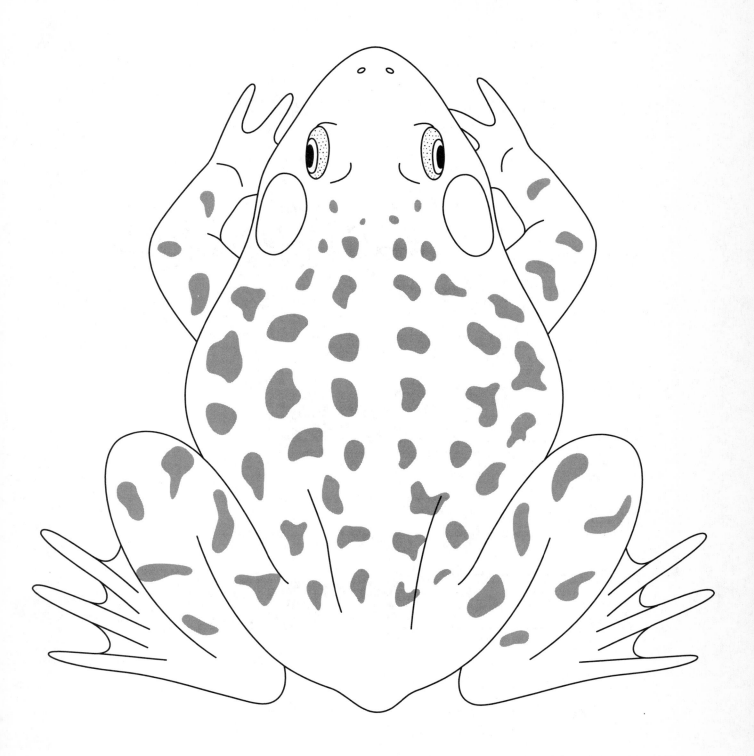

Use small frogs.
Record your work.

Name _____

How many frogs long is each 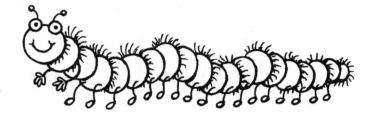 ?
Guess. Use frogs to measure.

A. Guess _____

Measure _____

B. Guess _____

Measure _____

C. Guess _____

Measure _____

EXPLORE MORE

Measure again. Use medium frogs.
Measure again. Use large frogs.

ACTIVITY 2

**Use medium frogs.
Record your work.**

Name _____

A. How long is your  ?

Guess. Use frogs to measure.

Guess_____ Measure_____

B. How long are your  ?

Guess. Use frogs to measure.

Guess_____ Measure_____

C. How long is your  ?

Guess. Use frogs to measure.

Guess_____ Measure_____

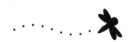

EXPLORE MORE

Compare your shoe to a friend's shoe. Are they about the same length? Guess. Use frogs to measure.

Use small frogs.
Record your work.

Name _____

Help Robbie Ribbit find the longer worm.

Which worm is longer?
Guess. Use frogs to measure.

	Guess	Measure
Worm A	_____	_____
Worm B	_____	_____

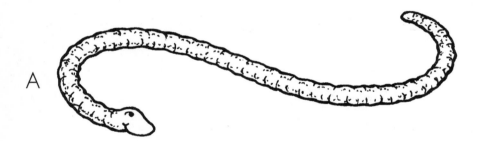

A

B

EXPLORE MORE
Measure again. Use medium frogs.
Measure again. Use large frogs.

Use small frogs.
Record your work.

Name _____

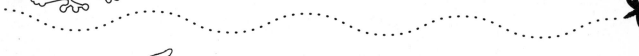

Trace your on the back of this paper.

A. How long is your ?

Guess. Use frogs to measure.

Guess_____ Measure_____

B. How long is your 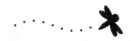 ?

Guess. Use frogs to measure.

Guess_____ Measure_____

EXPLORE MORE

Find something about as long as your .

Find something about as long as your _____ .

ACTIVITY 5

Use medium frogs.
Record your work.

Name _____

A. Find a book.
How long is the  ?

Guess. Use frogs to measure.

Guess_____ Measure_____

B. How wide is the  ?

Guess. Use frogs to measure.

Guess_____ Measure_____

c. Find something about as long as the  .
Use frogs to measure.
What did you find?_____

D. Find something about as wide as the
Use frogs to measure.
What did you find?_____

Name _____

Use small, medium, and large frogs.
Use a .
Record your work.

A. Hold a large frog in one hand.
Hold a small frog in the other hand.
Circle the frog that feels heavier.

Large   Small   Use the  to check.

B. Hold a medium frog in one hand.
Hold a large frog in the other hand.
Circle the frog that feels lighter.

 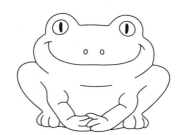

Medium   Large   Use the  to check.

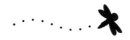

EXPLORE MORE

Find two frogs that feel the same.

Use the to check.

Use small frogs.
Use a .
Record your work.

Name _____

A. Compare these frogs.
Which group is heavier?

Guess. Use the [balance] to check.
Circle the heavier group.

Small	Small

B. Compare these frogs.
Which group is lighter?

Guess. Use the [balance] to check.
Circle the lighter group.

Small	Small

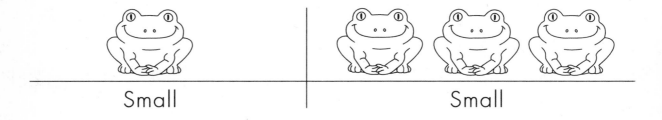

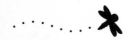

EXPLORE MORE
Balance the sides.
Make both sides the same.

Use medium frogs.
Use a .
Record your work.

Name _____

A. Compare these frogs.
Which group is heavier?

Guess. Use the [scale] to check.
Circle the heavier group.

Medium   Medium

B. Compare these frogs.
Which group is lighter?

Guess. Use the [scale] to check.
Circle the lighter group.

Medium   Medium

         0-7424-2770-6 *Funtastic Frogs™ Math Volume 1*

Use large frogs.
Use a 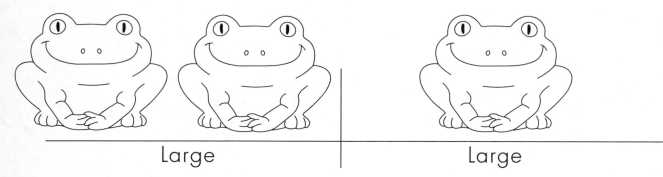.
Record your work.

Name _____

A. Compare these frogs.
Which group is heavier?

Guess. Use the ⬚ to check.
Circle the heavier group.

Large | Large

B. Compare these frogs.
Which group is lighter?

Guess. Use the ⬚ to check.
Circle the lighter group.

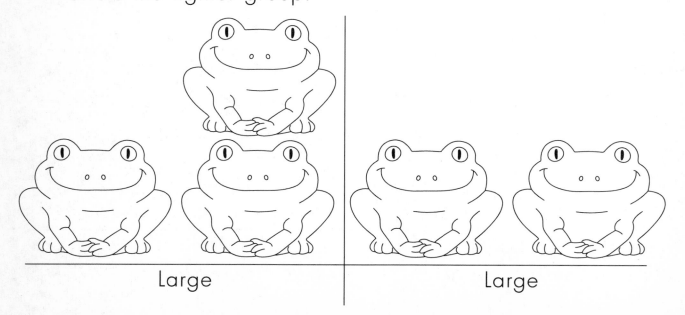

Large | Large

ACTIVITY 10

Name _____

Use small, medium, and large frogs.
Use a  .
Record your work.

A. How many small frogs will balance your pencil?
Guess. Use frogs to measure.

Guess_____

Measure_____

B. Find other things to balance.
Guess how many small frogs will balance each thing.
Use the [balance] to check.

Name of thing	Guess	Measure

EXPLORE MORE

Measure again. Use medium frogs.
Measure again. Use large frogs.

Use small frogs.
Record your work.

Name _____

A. How many frogs is it around the outside of this picture? Guess. Use frogs to measure.

Guess _____

Measure _____

B. How many frogs is it around the outside of this picture? Guess. Use frogs to measure.

Guess _____

Measure _____

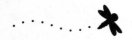

TALK ABOUT IT
Why are the numbers different?

Use medium frogs.
Record your work.

Name _____

A. How many frogs is it around the outside of Connie Croak's swimming pool?
Guess. Use frogs to measure.

Guess _____

Measure _____

B. How many frogs is it around the outside of Lori Leap's log?
Guess. Use frogs to measure.

Guess _____ Measure _____

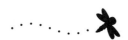

TALK ABOUT IT
Why are numbers different?

ACTIVITY **13**

Use large frogs.
Record your work.

Name _____

A. How many frogs is it around the outside of this book?
Guess. Use frogs to measure.

Guess_____

Measure_____

B. Find a book.
How many frogs is it around the outside of the book?
Guess. Use frogs to measure.

Guess_____

Measure_____

Use small, medium, large frogs. Record your work.

Name _____

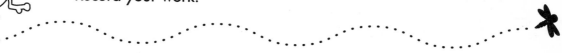

A. How many small frogs is it around the outside of Toad's house?

Guess_____   Measure_____

B. How many medium frogs is it around the outside of Toad's house?

Guess_____   Measure_____

C. How many large frogs is it around the outside of Toad's house?

Guess_____   Measure_____

TALK ABOUT IT
Why are the numbers different?

Name _____

Use small and large frogs.
Record your work.

A. How many small frogs is
it around the outside of
your desk?

Guess _____

Measure _____

B. How many large frogs is it around the outside of your desk?

Guess _____

Measure _____

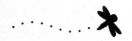

TALK ABOUT IT

Why are the numbers different?

ACTIVITY 16

Use small frogs.
Record your work.

Name _____

A. How many frogs will cover the ?
Guess. Use frogs to measure.

Guess_____

Measure_____

B. How many frogs will cover the ⊛ ?
Guess. Use frogs to measure.

Guess_____

Measure_____

TALK ABOUT IT
Why are the numbers different?

Use medium frogs.
Record your work.

Name _____

A. How many frogs will cover the 🌸?
Guess. Use frogs to measure.

Guess_____

Measure_____

B. How many frogs will cover the 🥒?
Guess. Use frogs to measure.

Guess_____   Measure_____

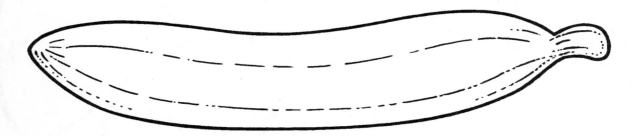

EXPLORE MORE

Measure again. Use small frogs.
Why are the numbers different?

       0-7424-2770-6 Funtastic Frogs™ Math Volume 1

Name _____

Use large frogs.
Record your work.

A. How many frogs will cover the  ?
Guess. Use frogs to measure.

Guess_____

Measure_____

B. How many frogs will cover the  ?
Guess. Use frogs to measure.

Guess_____   Measure_____

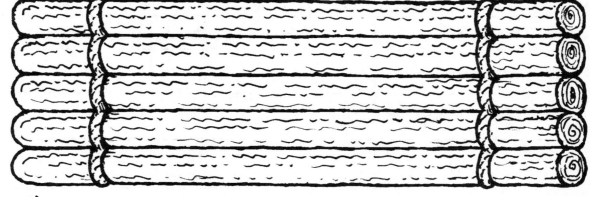

EXPLORE MORE

Measure again. Use small frogs.
Measure again. Use medium frogs.
Why are the numbers different?

ACTIVITY 19

Use small, medium, and large frogs. Record your work.

Name _____

How many frogs will cover the house?
Guess. Use frogs to measure.
Record your work in the chart.

Frog Size	Guess	Measure
Small Frogs		
Medium Frogs		
Large Frogs		

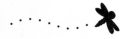

TALK ABOUT IT

Why are the numbers different?

Use small, medium, and large frogs. Record your work.

Name _____

How many frogs will cover the bus?
Guess. Use frogs to measure.
Record your work in the chart.

Frog Size	Guess	Measure
Small Frogs		
Medium Frogs		
Large Frogs		

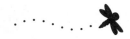

TALK ABOUT IT
Why are the numbers different?

Use small frogs and
a copy of page 105.
Record your work.

Name _____

The bullfrog is one of the largest frogs in the world.
Measure the picture of the bullfrog.
Find out how big a bullfrog can be.

A. How many frogs long is the bullfrog?
Guess. Use frogs to measure.

Guess_____   Measure_____

B. How many frogs is it around the outside of the bullfrog?

Guess_____   Measure_____

C. How many frogs will cover the bullfrog?

Guess_____   Measure_____

EXPLORE MORE
Find out more about bullfrogs.
Use the Internet and the library.

Use crayons or
colored markers,
scissors, and paste.

Name _____

Make a ruler.

Color the frogs.
Cut them out.
Paste the frogs on the shape.
Cut out the shape.

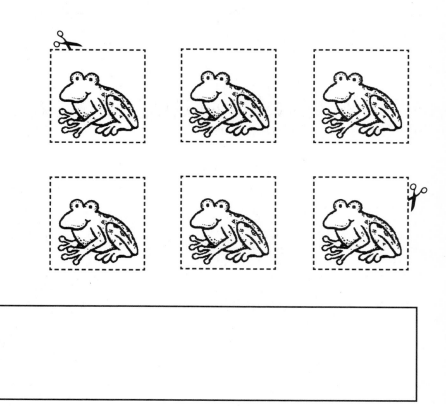

USE YOUR RULER
Find three things about as long as your ruler.

INVESTIGATION

**Use the Frog Ruler.
Record your work.**

Name _____

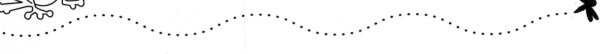

Use your Frog Ruler to measure.

A. Find two things about six frogs long.
Write what you found.

_____   _____

B. Find two things about four frogs long.
Write what you found.

_____   _____

C. Find two things about two frogs long.
Write what you found.

_____   _____

EXPLORE MORE
Use your Frog Ruler.
Find something about 12 frogs long.
Find something about 18 frogs long.

Use the bullfrog picture, string, and scissors.

Name _____

Bullfrogs can jump nine times their length.
How long is that leap?
Find a starting point.
Guess how far the bullfrog could jump.
Mark the end of the jump with a frog counter.
Use the bullfrog picture to measure.

How far could you leap if you were a frog?
Measure your body with a string.
Find a starting point.
Guess how far you could jump.
Mark the end of your jump with the bullfrog.
Use the string to measure your jump.

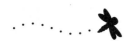

EXPLORE MORE
If you could jump like a frog, what would you do?

FUNtastic FROGS™

Making Patterns

Unit V

In Unit V, *Making Patterns,* children use the frog counters to:
- copy patterns
- identify patterns
- extend patterns
- predict patterns
- use patterns to solve problems

The activities in this unit are designed to teach that a pattern is a sequence of objects that repeats over and over. Children learn that they can use patterns to predict what comes next and to solve problems.

Working with patterns is key to the development of a child's mathematical thinking. It provides a framework for recognizing the patterns in our number system. It helps children develop their ability to make generalizations, think logically, and solve problems in mathematics. Early experiences with patterns develop skills that are needed for work with functions and algebra in the later years. All the activities in this unit support current mathematics standards.

Contents
This unit contains 22 activities divided into sections on copying, describing, predicting, and completing patterns. Each section features activities that are similar, giving children the opportunity to practice and refine their skills.

Sample solutions are provided on pages 136 and 137.

Math Skills and Understandings	Related Activities
Represent patterns using concrete objects	Activities 1–22
Identify, describe, copy, and extend a pattern	Activities 1–22
Translate patterns	Activities 1–12
Predict a pattern	Activities 1–12
Use patterns to solve problems	Activities 18–22

Suggestions for Classroom Use

Encourage children to share their thinking with the whole class. Talking about their thinking helps children clarify their thoughts and allows others to hear how they might solve the same problem a different way. Talking about how they solve problems helps children make mathematical connections and deepens their understanding. Class discussions encourage the type of thinking required for reasoning and problem solving.

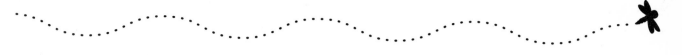

Materials

You may wish to make an overhead transparency of the first activity page in each section as an introduction to the activities that follow.

For each child, pair of children, or group, you will need:
- pencils
- crayons or colored markers to match the colors of the frogs
- a tub of frogs in three sizes and six colors
- an activity sheet for each child or pair of children

If children are not able to record by writing numbers and coloring, make copies of page 138. The children can color and cut out the frogs, then paste or glue them in place to record.

Introducing the Activities
When you introduce a section of the unit, lead the children through the first activity in that section. Discuss the directions and how to record their work. When reviewing an activity as a group, encourage the children to talk about their discoveries. This will help them make connections and clarify their thinking.

Mathematical Content by Section

Activities 1–12: Copying, describing, extending, predicting, and translating patterns.
This series of activities is divided into three sections. Activities 1–4 focus on ABAB patterns; activities 5–8 focus on ABBABB patterns; and activities 9–12 focus on ABCABC patterns. Each section of four activities is structured the same way.

Distribute the first activity of the section. Model making the first pattern. Point out that a pattern is something that repeats again and again in the same way. Ask questions such as: *What are some things you can tell me about this pattern? How can we describe this pattern?* Demonstrate how to "read" or say the pattern using terms supplied by the children. Ask: *How can we record this pattern?* Children may suggest using colors, words, letters, or numbers.

As you begin the second activity in each section, note that the patterns are built from the bottom to the top. Review the directions and model the first pattern if necessary. Ask questions such as: *What is the pattern? Can you read it to me? What part keeps repeating? What makes it a pattern?*

The third activity in each section requires the children to predict the missing part of the pattern in each row. Point out the pattern on the page and ask: *How is this pattern like the one we did before? What is the pattern? Who thinks they know how to find the missing part?*

In the fourth activity of each section, the children apply what they have learned about the pattern. The first time the children do this activity (Activity 4), model the first problem on the page, then have the children complete the page.

Activities 13–17: Completing patterns to identify a color in an ordinal position.
Introduce the first part of Activity 13 to the whole class. Read the directions, and model making the first pattern. Ask: *Can you name this pattern?* To check for understanding, ask: *What is the pattern? Can you read it to me? What part keeps repeating?* Review the ordinal positions with the children. Ask: *What is the color of the first frog? What is the color of the third frog?* and so on.

Activities 18–22: Using patterns to solve a problem.
Children must look for the patterns and use problem-solving skills to fill in the puzzles on these pages. Before you go through Activity 18, set up the pattern in an extended line, using frog counters and leaving blank spaces where indicated:

Ask children to identify the pattern, then to complete it by putting the missing frogs in place. Then, keeping the frogs in the same order, rearrange them in three rows of three:

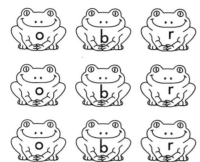

Help children see that the pattern remains the same when the frogs are in rows or in a line. When you get to the end of a line, you just continue the pattern on the next line.

Work through Activity 18 with the children. To check for understanding, ask questions such as: *How can we tell this is a repeating pattern? How can we use the pattern to find the missing frog colors?* Guide the children to complete the pattern. Go over the directions for each of the following pattern puzzles before assigning them to the children.

When you get to Activity 20, you might show the pattern in a line, then in the grid. Help children see that when they get to the end of a line, they can continue the pattern on the next line.

Ideas for Extending the Learning
- Invite the children to extend the pattern of an activity.
- Act out patterns with physical movements.
- Make up auditory patterns for the children to copy and extend.
- Invite the children to listen for patterns in music or poetry.
- Provide different materials for children to use to record patterns, such as paint, paper, cereal, or pasta pieces.
- Children can use laces or string to make frog pattern necklaces to wear for the day.
- Ask children to look for patterns in the real world. Point out that they can find patterns on clothing, in the play yard, on buildings, at home, and almost anywhere.
- Display the children's recordings of patterns for everyone to enjoy.

Sample Solutions for This Unit

These are sample solutions. Additional solutions are possible for some activities.

Activity

1A. purple, green pattern **1B.** blue, red pattern

2A. yellow, blue pattern **2B.** green, orange pattern

3A. blue **3B.** red, yellow **3C.** green, yellow, green

4A. blue, red, blue, red, blue, red
    3 blue frogs
    3 red frogs
4B. green, purple, green, purple, green, purple
    3 green frogs
    3 purple frogs

5A. red, yellow, yellow **5B.** blue, orange, orange
5C. red, blue, blue

6A. blue, green, green **6B.** yellow, red, red

7A. orange **7B.** blue, blue **7C.** blue, yellow, yellow

8A. purple, green, green, purple, green, green
    2 purple frogs
    4 green frogs
8B. blue, green, green, blue, green, green
    2 blue frogs
    4 green frogs

9A. red, blue, yellow, red, blue, yellow
9B. green, orange, purple, green, orange, purple
9C.   orange, yellow, green, orange, yellow, green

10A. red, yellow, blue, red, yellow, blue
10B. yellow, green, purple, yellow, green, purple

11A. purple **11B.** yellow, blue **11C.** purple, yellow, green

12A. blue, red, purple, blue, red, purple
    2 blue
    2 red
    2 purple
12B. yellow, green, orange, yellow, green, orange
    2 yellow
    2 green
    2 orange

13A. yellow **13B.** orange **13C.** green, orange

14A. red **14B.** purple **14C.** blue, green, green

15A. orange **15B.** blue
15C. yellow, orange, green

16A. green **16B.** blue
16C. green, orange, yellow

17A. red **17B.** green

18

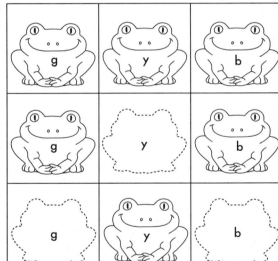

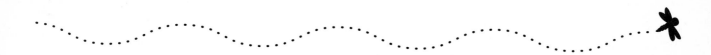

Sample Solutions

These are sample solutions. Additional solutions are possible for some activities.

Activity

19

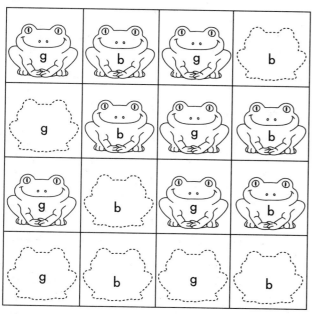

Activity

21

20

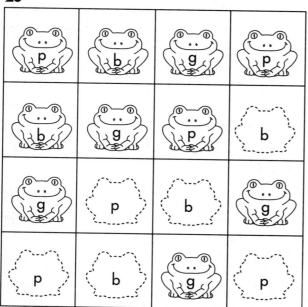

22

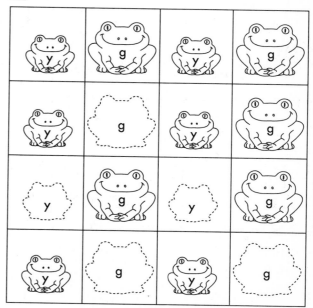

138

 Copy a pattern

ACTIVITY 1

Use small frogs.
Record your work.

Name _____

Match the frogs.
Name the pattern.
Color to record.

A.

B.

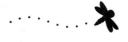

EXPLORE MORE

Make your own pattern.

ACTIVITY 2

Use medium frogs.
Record your work.

Name _____

Match the frogs.
Name the pattern.
Color to record.

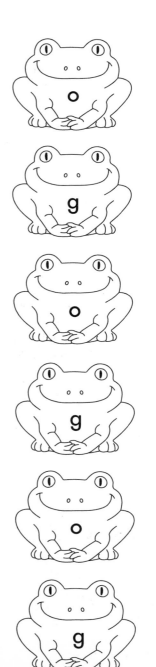

A.   B.

ACTIVITY 3

Use small frogs.
Record your work.

Name _____

Match the frogs.
Complete the pattern.
Color to record.

A.

g   b   g   b   g

B.

r   y   r   y

C.

y   g   y

Use small frogs.
Record your work.

Name _____

A. Use blue and red frogs.
Make a blue, red pattern.
Color to record.

How many blue frogs? _____

How many red frogs? _____

B. Use green and purple frogs.
Make a green, purple pattern.
Color to record.

How many green frogs? _____

How many purple frogs? _____

Name _____

Use small frogs.
Record your work.

Match the frogs.
Name the pattern.
Color to record.

A.

B.

C.

ACTIVITY 6

Use medium frogs.
Record your work.

Name _____

Match the frogs.
Name the pattern.
Color to record.

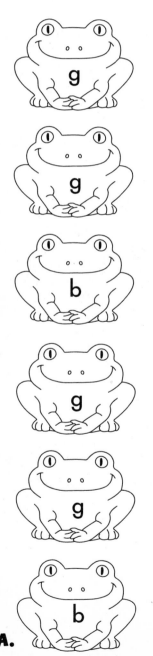

g
g
b
g
g
b

A.

r
r
y
r
r
y

B.

**Use small frogs.
Record your work.**

Name _____

Match the frogs.
Complete the pattern.
Color to record.

A.

B.

C.

Use small frogs.
Record your work.

A. Use purple and green frogs.
Make a purple, green, green pattern.
Color to record.

How many purple frogs? _____

How many green frogs? _____

B. Use blue and green frogs.
Make a blue, green, green pattern.
Color to record.

How many blue frogs? _____

How many green frogs? _____

Use small frogs.
Record your work.

Name _____

Match the frogs.
Name the pattern.
Color to record.

A.

B.

C.

Use medium frogs.
Record your work.

Name _____

Match the frogs.
Name the pattern.
Color to record.

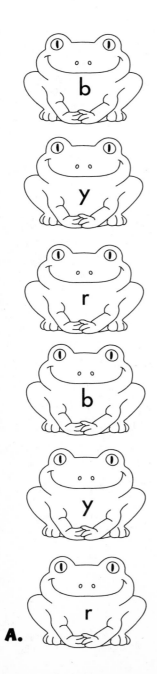

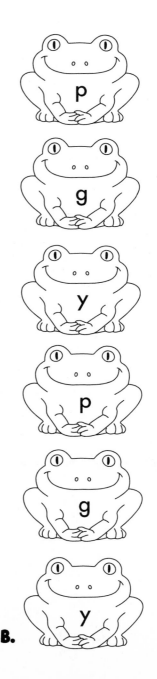

**Use small frogs.
Record your work.**

Name _____

Match the frogs.
Complete the pattern.
Color to record.

A.

B.

C.

0-7424-2770-6 Funtastic Frogs™ Math Volume 1

A. Use blue, red, and purple frogs.
Use all the colors to make a pattern.
Color to record.

How many blue frogs? _____

How many red frogs? _____

How many purple frogs? _____

B. Use yellow, green, and orange frogs.
Use all the colors to make a pattern.
Color to record.

How many yellow frogs? _____

How many green frogs? _____

How many orange frogs? _____

Use small frogs.
Record your work.

Name _____

Match the frogs.
Color to record.

A.

What color is the first frog?_____

B.

What color is the second frog?_____

C. Color the first frog green.
Color the second frog orange.
Continue the pattern.

Use small frogs.
Record your work.

Match the frogs.
Color to record.

A.

What color is the third frog?_____

B.

What color is the fourth frog?_____

C. Color the third frog green.
Color the fourth frog blue.
Continue the pattern.

0-7424-2770-6 Funtastic Frogs™ Math Volume 1

ACTIVITY 15

Use small frogs.
Record your work.

Name _____

Match the frogs.
Color to record.

A.

p   o   g   p   o   g

What color is the fifth frog?_____

B.

r   y   b   r   y   b

What color is the sixth frog?_____

C. Color the fifth frog orange.
Color the sixth frog green.
Complete the pattern.

y   o   g

0-7424-2770-6 Funtastic Frogs™ Math Volume 1

ACTIVITY **16**

Use small frogs.
Record your work.

Match the frogs.
Continue the pattern.
Color to record.

A.

What color is the fourth frog?_____

B.

What color is the sixth frog?_____

C. Color the fifth frog orange.
Color the sixth frog yellow.
Complete the pattern.

Use small frogs.
Record your work.

Name _____

Match the frogs.
Continue the pattern.
Color to record.

A.

What color will the tenth frog be?_____

B.

What color will the tenth frog be?_____

Use large frogs.
Record your work.

Name _____

Match the frogs.
Use the pattern to fill in the puzzle.
Color to record.

Name _____

Use medium frogs.
Record your work.

Match the frogs.
Use the pattern to fill in the puzzle.
Color to record.

Use small frogs.
Record your work.

Name _____

Match the frogs.
Use the pattern to fill in the puzzle.
Color to record.

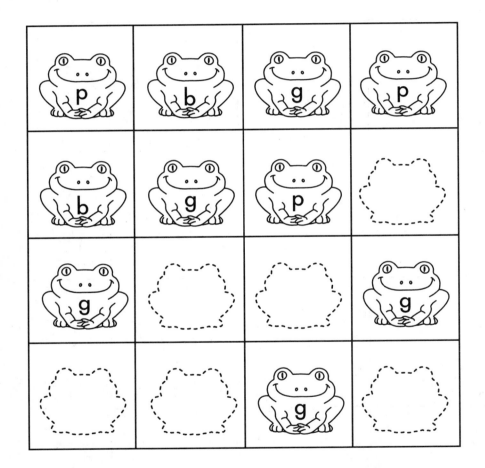

ACTIVITY 21

Name _____

Use small frogs.
Record your work.

Match the frogs.
Use the pattern to fill in the puzzle.
Color to record.

b	r	r	b
r	r	b	
r	b	r	
	r	r	b

ACTIVITY 22

Use small and
medium frogs.
Record your work.

Name _____

Match the frogs.
Use the pattern to fill in the puzzle.
Color to record.